Praise for *GRO*

"This book really captures the essence of 'working together' to define a compelling vision, comprehensive strategy, and relentless implementation plan to deliver profitable growth for all the company's stakeholders!"

Alan Mulally
Former President/CEO
Ford Motor Company

"It's a must-read for every business owner who wonders how to get out of their own way and get the right resources to grow."

Gino Wickman
Author of the award-winning book *Traction*
Creator of EOS Worldwide

"This quick read is a must-read for every business owner who wants to grow! Two likeable thumbs up!"

Dave Kerpen
New York Times Bestselling Author
The Art of People

"If you are an entrepreneur, owner, or CEO who has matured enough to finally realize you only have a finite number of days in your life, and you really want to capture these to their fullest, then read this simple book. It is a 'can't miss' formula that my clients have been following for years."

Walt Brown
Multi-Company Entrepreneur
Seasoned Coach and Peer Board Facilitator
Expert EOS Implementer™

"This book is a key tool for any entrepreneur looking for growth or solutions to everyday challenges that come with leading a company."

Amilya M. Antonetti
CEO AmA Productions

"As a Vistage Chair, I have shared over 25 clients with EOS Implementers. These concepts have helped my Vistage CEOs share a common language, provide real-time case studies of success, and optimize their businesses with the power of EOS tools, peer advisory boards, and executive coaching. More importantly, it helps my CEOs become significantly more successful while working fewer hours so that they can enjoy their lives, businesses, and families."

Jonathan Jones
Vistage Master Chair

"Time and again, I've seen the magic unfold when leaders step boldly into clarifying their vision, leveling up accountability, and nourishing their teams with genuine care. When entrepreneurial organizations leverage the power of business operating systems, like EOS, with peer/industry groups and individual leadership coaching, growth isn't just possible—it becomes inevitable. The ripple effects strengthen not only the business but every single person within it. That's the magic I love to witness, create, and champion every day."

Jill Young
Author of the *Advantage* book series
Host of the *Coaching Magic* podcast

"*GROW!* is a masterclass in combining operational excellence, peer wisdom, and coaching insight. Every time our Leadership Council members engage with all three, they have break-throughs, which they then share with their fellow members in a ripple effect of insight and wisdom. This is the kind of business and personal growth that only happens with holistic support."

Amy Scharff
President, Leadership Council

GROW!

*How Entrepreneurial Leaders
Optimize for Growth*

GROW!

*How Entrepreneurial Leaders
Optimize for Growth*

JONATHAN B. SMITH
AND
JEANET L. WADE

EOS
IMPACT

Printed in the United States of America

Published by Igniting Souls
PO Box 43, Powell, OH 43065
IgnitingSouls.com

LCCN: 2025917082
Paperback ISBN: 978-1-63680-562-7
Hardback ISBN: 978-63680-563-4
eBook ISBN: 978-62680-564-1

Available in paperback, hardcover, e-book, and audiobook.

Any Internet addresses (websites, blogs, etc.) and telephone numbers printed in this book are offered as a resource. They are not intended in any way to be or imply an endorsement by Igniting Souls, nor does Igniting Souls vouch for the content of these sites and numbers for the life of this book.

Some names and identifying details may have been changed to protect the privacy of individuals.

The content of this book reflects the author's personal experiences, opinions, and interpretations. The inclusion of any individual, living or deceased, or any organization or entity, is not intended to malign, defame, or harm the reputation of such persons or entities. All statements regarding individuals are solely the author's perspective and do not represent verified facts unless expressly cited to a verifiable source.

The publisher has not independently investigated or confirmed the accuracy of any such references and disclaims all responsibility for them. Nothing in this book should be construed as factual assertions about the character, conduct, or reputation of any individual or entity mentioned. Any resemblance to persons living or dead is purely coincidental unless explicitly stated.

The publisher expressly disclaims liability for any alleged loss, damage, or injury arising from any perceived defamatory content or reliance upon statements within this work. Responsibility for the views, depictions, and representations rests solely with the author.

EOS®, The Entrepreneurial Operating System®, Traction®, and EOS Implementer® are registered trademarks owned by EOS Worldwide, LLC. For a complete list of trademarks owned by EOS Worldwide throughout this book, please visit branding.eosworldwide.com/eos-trademarks/.

The superscript symbol IP listed throughout this book is known as the unique certification mark created and owned by Instant IP™. Its use signifies that the corresponding expression (words, phrases, chart, graph, etc.) has been protected by Instant IP™ via smart contract. Instant IP™ is designed with the patented smart contract solution (US Patent: 11,928,748), which creates an immutable time-stamped first layer and fast layer identifying the moment in time an idea is filed on the blockchain. This solution can be used in defending intellectual property protection. Infringing upon the respective intellectual property, i.e., IP, is subject to and punishable in a court of law.

TABLE OF CONTENTS

FOREWORD BY MARK O'DONNELL

When I look back on my entrepreneurial journey—from launching my first business with my brother, to building a company that landed on the Inc. 5000 list five years in a row, to now serving as Visionary at EOS Worldwide—I see a common thread: the power of optimizing for growth by surrounding myself with the right people, systems, and support.

Early in my career, I thought growth was all about hustle and having the best ideas. But as my companies scaled, I hit the same ceiling so many leaders face—overwhelm, lack of clarity, and the realization that I couldn't do it alone. It was during this period that I discovered the principles at the heart of *Grow! How Entrepreneurial Leaders Optimize for Growth*. I learned that real, sustainable growth happens when you implement a company operating system, tap into a community of peers, and work with a coach who challenges you to become your best self.

When my own business was growing rapidly, I was introduced to EOS. Implementing EOS didn't just bring discipline and structure; it fundamentally shifted how I led. Suddenly, I had a clear vision, real accountability, and a healthy, aligned team. But the real magic happened when I combined EOS with the wisdom of peer groups and the guidance of executive coaches. That combination helped me 8x my net worth, and, more importantly, allowed me to spend my days doing what I love, with people I love, making a difference in the world. This ecosystem of support has shaped every major decision I've made since.

At EOS Worldwide, we don't just teach operating systems—we live the values of community and coaching. We believe in abundance: that there's more than enough success to go around, and that when we help others grow, we all rise together. Our global community of Implementers, coaches, and entrepreneurial leaders is built on the idea that collaboration, not competition, creates mastery. We see firsthand how leaders who embrace a peer network and seek out coaching accelerate their growth, gain confidence, and create healthier, more valuable businesses.

This book captures that formula for growth. It's not just about EOS or any single system—it's about building an ecosystem where **company** operating systems, **community** peer groups, and **coaching** work in harmony. That's how you break through ceilings, unlock your full potential, and create abundance for yourself, your team, and your clients.

If you're ready to grow—not just your business, but your impact and your life—read on. The roadmap is here.

—Mark O'Donnell, CEO and Visionary, EOS Worldwide

INTRODUCTION: OPTIMIZE FOR GROWTH

Every entrepreneurial leader faces the same fundamental challenge: how to break through growth ceilings and scale their business sustainably. After working with hundreds of companies as Expert EOS Implementers and witnessing countless transformations, we've discovered a powerful truth that changes everything: the most successful entrepreneurial leaders don't rely on heroic effort alone—they optimize for growth by implementing **three critical support systems** that work in harmony.

Through our combined experience helping businesses scale, we've developed what we call the "Optimize for Growth Model."[1] This model consists of three interconnected elements:

1. A **COMPANY** operating system (sometimes called an organizational or business operating system) that creates organizational clarity and accountability

2. A **COMMUNITY** of peers that provides an external perspective and wisdom

3. A **COACH** who develops individual leadership capabilities

When these three elements work together, the results are extraordinary.

The Optimize for Growth Model: Three interconnected elements driving business success

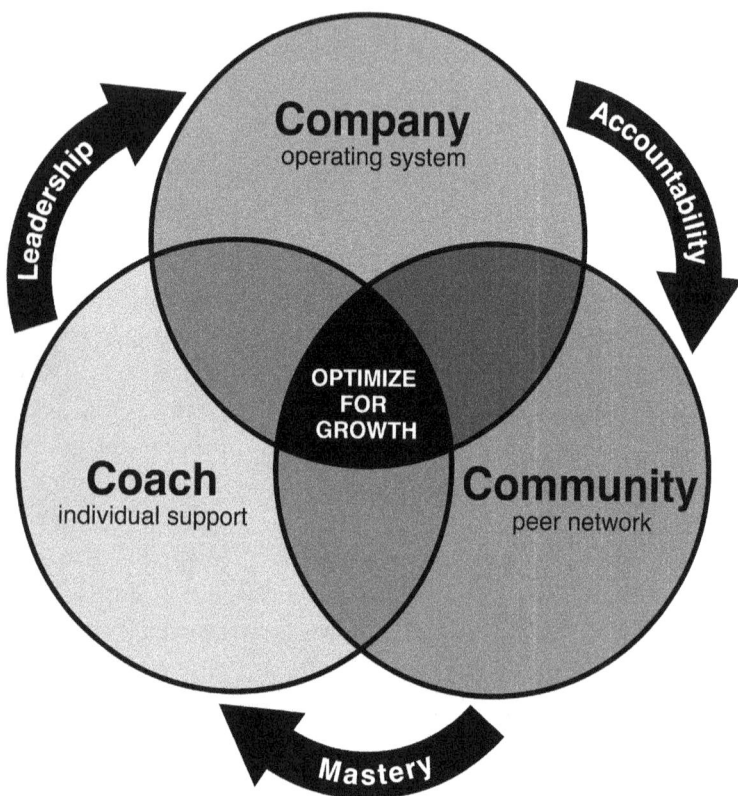

This isn't theory—it's proven methodology backed by real results. We've seen service companies grow from $3 million to $15 million in three years, manufacturing businesses scale from $8 million to $25 million in four years, and consulting firms accelerate from $500,000 to $5 million in just 2.5 years. The common thread? They didn't grow alone.

Peer advisory groups have been shown to lead to real business gains—participants achieve more than two times the average growth and profit rates of their industry.[2] Executive coaching also has a powerful impact, with 86 percent of clients reporting a positive ROI from improvements in decision-making, communication, work performance, and organizational effectiveness. When combined with a proven company operating system like EOS®, the Entrepreneurial Operating System®, which has helped over 280,000 businesses worldwide gain traction on their vision, the results compound exponentially.

But here's what makes this approach truly revolutionary: it's not just about what these elements do individually—it's about how they work together. A company operating system provides the foundational tools, systems, and processes to run a more effective organization; peer advisory groups offer a strategic perspective; and executive coaching develops the personal leadership capabilities needed to guide growth.

Each element amplifies the others, creating what we call the "optimization effect."

In this book, we'll share the exact framework we've used to help hundreds of entrepreneurial leaders break through their growth ceilings. You'll discover how to select the right operating system, find the perfect peer advisory group, and choose a coach who can accelerate your development. More importantly, you'll learn how to integrate these elements to create a growth engine that scales with your business.

HITTING THE CEILING: WHEN GOOD COMPANIES GET STUCK

The owner of a packaging company once came to us with a frustrating dilemma: He had built his business from nothing to $2 million in revenue, but he couldn't figure out how to get beyond that. He wanted to reach $5 million, but despite working eighteen-hour days, the grit and determination that built his business weren't moving the needle anymore. He told us, "I'm good at selling and plowing through work and making things happen, but I'm not the best at managing people and staying on top of them to make sure work gets done. No one knows what their roles are, and financially, it's a mess."

He was learning the hard truth: *scale-up is much harder than start-up.* Every entrepreneur confronts this reality eventually, usually when they least expect it. We've witnessed this scenario countless times, where a visionary entrepreneur builds a successful company through sheer determination and creativity, only to find themselves trapped by the very success they created.

His experience illustrates what's known as the "founder's paradox."[3] The entrepreneurial skills that create a business—vision, drive, and personal involvement in every detail—become limitations when trying to scale. This transition from startup to scale-up creates predictable barriers that the vast majority of growing companies encounter. Here are the roadblocks we see most often in scaling companies, why they're so common, and why startups are rarely equipped to overcome them.

The Five Critical Roadblocks

Through our work implementing EOS and coaching entrepreneurial leaders, we've identified five primary barriers that consistently prevent growth.

People Problems: Leaders become frustrated with employees, customers, vendors, and partners. Nobody seems to listen, understand, or follow through consistently. Teams struggle with dysfunction due to unclear roles, limited accountability, and poor communication. A study by Gallup found that only 15 percent of employees worldwide feel engaged at work, directly impacting productivity and growth.[4]

Profit Pressures: The business fails to generate adequate profit to justify the time and effort required. Leaders lack sufficient working capital for daily operations and often resort to debt financing to cover shortfalls. According to the Small Business Administration, cash flow problems cause 82 percent of business failures.[5]

Control Crisis: Leaders feel they've lost control over their time, market position, or company direction. Instead of controlling the business, the business controls them. One recent survey found that 78 percent of CEOs felt a high level of business uncertainty, which some struggle to handle.[6]

Nothing Works: Organizations have tried multiple solutions—books, consultants, new ideas—but nothing creates lasting change. Teams develop "initiative fatigue" from constant change efforts that lack integration and sustainability. McKinsey research shows that 70 percent of organizational change efforts fail, often due to a lack of a systematic approach.[7]

Traction Deficiency: Leaders spend more time firefighting than building sustainable growth through disciplined, repeatable processes. They can't gain consistent momentum toward their vision while maintaining team health. According to *Harvard Business Review*, the failure to develop and execute these processes is one of the top risks to business survival.[8]

A Sustainable Legacy

For Alex Fechner, the family business is more than just a legacy; it's a calling. As a fourth-generation leader of Advertisers Printing, Alex grew up immersed in the world of print, spending weekends at the plant and learning every facet of the operation from the ground up.

But times change, and with the digital revolution threatening the survival of many printers, Alex couldn't afford to keep doing things the same way as always. He needed a way to embrace innovation without losing sight of the company's core values—and he knew he couldn't do it alone.

To stay relevant in a rapidly changing business environment, he turned to experts and peers for help. By implementing the Entrepreneurial Operating System, engaging with experienced coaches, and staying active in peer advisory networks, Alex and his team built a culture of continuous improvement and accountability. These strategies have helped Advertisers Printing achieve remarkable results—including a 28 percent increase in revenue in 2022—while fostering a workplace where creativity, sustainability, and client success are paramount.

Alex credits EOS and the company's commitment to community for helping Advertisers Printing adapt to changing markets, launch successful omnichannel cam

---

paigns, and develop new leaders from within. "Print is in my blood," Alex says. "We're not just making beautiful pieces—we're building relationships and driving results for our clients. Thanks to the systems and support we've put in place, we're proving every day that print is far from dead— it's evolving, and so are we."

Today, he's at the forefront of a company that's been serving St. Louis businesses for over a century, proving that print is not only alive but thriving in the digital age.

Breakthrough Skills

As frustrating as it is to see your growth stall, it's normal. As Harvard's "Evolution and Revolution" framework explains, business growth isn't linear—it requires both incremental improvements (evolution) and fundamental transformations (revolution).[9] When growth flattens, it's time for a revolution. According to Gino Wickman (author of *Traction* & *Shine* and founder of EOS), entrepreneurial leaders must develop five critical abilities to break through growth ceilings.

Simplify: The ability to focus on fewer priorities while accomplishing more, reducing organizational complexity and chaos. Research by Jim Collins shows that companies with disciplined focus outperform their peers by a factor of ten.[10]

Delegate: The ability to leverage collective human effort by getting support from the right people in appropriate roles. Research has found that CEOs who effectively delegate grow their companies 33 percent faster than those who don't.[11]

Predict: The ability to make both short-term and long-term predictions that drive growth decisions. According to research by McKinsey, strong forecasting capabilities are a key factor in the long-term resilience of a business.[12]

Systemize: The ability to create processes that add value beyond the entrepreneur's personal involvement. According to Bain & Company, businesses with documented, repeatable processes scale faster and more reliably than those dependent on individual heroics.[13]

Structure: The ability to design organizational architecture that puts the right people in the right seats. Research shows that companies with optimal organizational design achieve higher productivity, agility, and profitability.[14]

Looking Beyond Internal Resources

As companies transition from start-up to scale-up, the demands of the business often surpass the internal team's ability to keep up. When it comes to capacity, skills, and expertise, there's a gap between where the team is and where they need to be to take full advantage of the growth opportunities at hand. That makes sense—most founders haven't yet operated large businesses, and their teams are typically small and relatively inexperienced.

To bridge that gap, smart leaders leverage external expertise. They seek out trusted experts who can act like temporary support columns in construction, providing stability while internal capabilities develop. This approach allows organizations to "take the elevator instead of the stairs"—to grow faster with less effort.

Digital Strike, a digital marketing agency founded by Chris Westmeyer, is a perfect example of this. Between 2010 and 2018, the company grew steadily, earning a coveted spot on the Inc. 5000 list in 2018. But by 2019, it hit a plateau. Growth slowed, challenges mounted, and Chris and his leadership team realized that what had gotten them this far wouldn't take them to the next level.

"We needed a new solution—a framework to reignite growth and help us address emerging challenges," Chris recalls. As they explored options and consulted with other business owners, one idea kept surfacing: EOS.

The journey to EOS was not a straight line. In 2019, Chris and his team dove into research, spoke with peers, and read foundational EOS books like *Traction, Rocket Fuel,* and *What the Heck is EOS?* They brought in new team members with EOS experience and interviewed potential implementers. In 2020, they committed fully and hired an EOS Implementer® who aligned with their culture and needs.

Despite their commitment, progress was slow at first. The leadership team struggled to gain traction with the new tools and disciplines that EOS required. "There were times we questioned whether EOS was the right solution for us," Chris admits. "Were we implementing it correctly? Was there a better framework out there?" Through persistence—and with the guidance of their implementer—they realized a critical missing piece: the Integrator (President) role. By the end of 2021, they had hired an Integrator, and the impact was almost immediate.

With the Integrator in place, Digital Strike began to see real change. The leadership team was restructured, new processes were created, and ambitious yet achievable goals were set. EOS provided the structure and clarity needed to thrive in the competitive digital marketing space.

One of the most significant benefits was in strategic leadership recruitment: their EOS Implementer leveraged their network to help identify and secure two key leadership hires, saving Digital Strike up to $80,000 in recruitment fees and countless hours in evaluation.

EOS also enabled Digital Strike to refine its business focus. Rather than trying to be all things to all clients, they honed their expertise into a select set of high-value, profitable services tailored to specific audiences. This strategic shift delivered measurable results, including 24 percent year-over-year growth in the first full year after implementation.

In addition to working with their EOS Implementer, the leaders at Digital Strike actively sought other external resources to help scaffold their growth as they developed their internal capabilities. They engaged in industry associations, participated in peer networks, and hired coaches and consultants to create a community of support for themselves and their clients. This network not only provided fresh perspectives and accountability but also helped Digital Strike stay ahead of digital trends and business best practices.

Today, Digital Strike is a testament to what's possible when a company looks beyond its internal resources. By leveraging external expertise to build a strong scaffold, the agency has not only escaped its plateau but has also built a culture of transparency, accountability, and continuous improvement. "EOS helped us regain momentum and provided the clarity and structure we needed to thrive," Chris says. "But it was our willingness to reach out, learn from others, and invest in our community that truly set us apart."

The Optimize for Growth Model

Digital Strike's story proves the power of the Optimize for Growth Model. They didn't just hire a lone advisor or focus on improving one part of the business. They developed a comprehensive support system with three crucial elements—the key elements for scaling successfully.

COMPANY: An operating system that enables the business to run at scale rather than depending on heroic founder efforts. This includes clear vision, systematic processes, and organizational accountability.

COMMUNITY: A trusted peer network that leverages collective wisdom, similar to a board of advisors. This provides an external perspective, strategic insights, and accountability from other successful leaders.

COACH: Individual support that develops leadership skills, addresses blind spots, and creates new approaches to self-improvement. This ensures that personal growth keeps pace with business growth.

Each element individually supports entrepreneurial growth. Together, they amplify results and improve your chances of success. Organizations that utilize multiple support systems achieve a better return on their investments, higher growth rates, and faster time to achieve the desired impact when these approaches are combined. We've personally seen the impact in our own businesses as well as those of our clients.

Due to one-on-one coaching, a peer advisory group, and a strong support community, Jeanet personally saw a 9.3x multiple on growth and spent 37 percent less time in her business from 2015 to 2020. These types of 3x to 10x growth rates and reduced busyness in the business are common when entrepreneurs and leaders optimize themselves and their companies.

It can be daunting to think about building this entire three-part support system. Fortunately, you can take it one step at a time, in whatever order makes sense for your business. Whether you work with an operating system implementer, join a peer group, or engage a coach first, you'll begin developing the discipline, structure, and team health necessary to break through your ceiling. Each element takes your business beyond internal limitations by connecting you with experts who have "been there and done that."

The system achieves two primary goals: providing access to trusted advisors and experts who help optimize growth and delivering necessary tools to tackle daily barriers to expansion. Each element drives specific types of growth—profit, leadership, and personal momentum—all of which are essential for business success.

Don't Hold Yourself Back

You're probably wondering if you *really* need to invest in all these different support systems. You're a busy business leader with lots of plates to spin and lots of bills to pay. Wouldn't it be enough to just invest your time and money in *one* of these three areas?

We hear this concern from skeptical executives all the time, and it's a red flag for the biggest obstacle that will get in the way of your growth: a scarcity mindset. Scarcity thinking is rooted in fear—in this case, fear of doing something different and not getting the payoff you expect. It seems safer and easier to just try a small tweak and see how far it takes you.

That's fine if you're just looking for a little boost. But if you want to break through a growth ceiling and finally achieve true scalability, small tweaks are not going to cut it. You don't just need to do the same things you've been doing, but more and better. You need to do something *different*. These three support systems, when working together, dramatically increase the chances that you'll make that brave choice and follow through on it.

So replace that scarcity thinking with a *growth orientation* and an *abundance mindset*. A growth orientation is a commitment to truly scale up in a big and sustainable way. An abundance mindset is the belief that when you invest your time, energy, and resources in the right things, you'll get them back many times over in the long run.

The journey begins now. **Let's grow!**

Chapter Takeaways

- Scale-up companies tend to hit the same five roadblocks to growth: people problems, profit pressures, control crisis, nothing works, and traction deficiency.

- To break through growth ceilings, entrepreneurial leaders must develop five critical breakthrough abilities: simplify, delegate, predict, systematize, and structure.

- Building those skills requires leaders to look beyond their internal resources for support.

- To optimize for maximum growth, that support should come from three sources:

  o A **company** operating system

  o A **community** of trusted peers

  o A **coach** for executive leaders

- Those three support systems mutually reinforce each other, so companies that use all of them grow faster and better than with just one.

[2]

OPTIMIZE YOUR COMPANY:
GET A GRIP ON YOUR BUSINESS

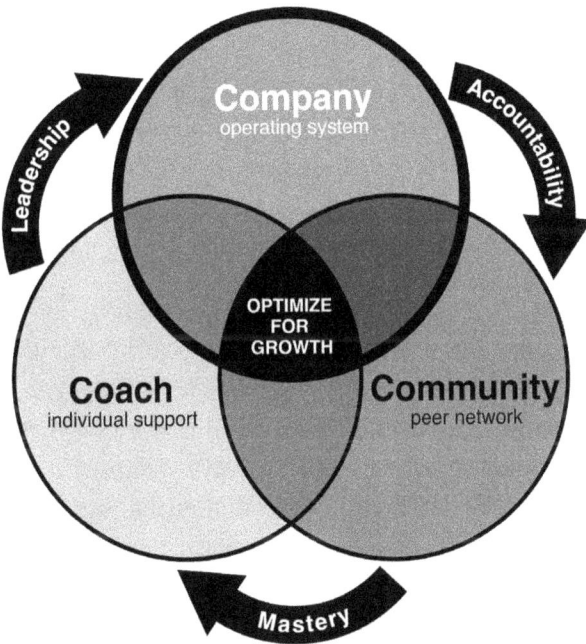

In 2001, Jonathan's first startup was on the verge of failure. Despite having a capable team and a clear market opportunity, 3D New Media had stalled, and Jonathan and his partners were struggling to understand why. So, they brought in Gino Wickman to diagnose the problem.[15]

Almost immediately, the issues became clear. The three partners were working at odds, each pursuing different priorities and doing things their own particular way. Instead of amplifying each other's efforts, they were duplicating work, undermining each other, and wasting precious time on internal conflicts.

As Gino dug deeper, he discovered the reason for all this friction: the partners didn't want the same things for the company or themselves. That made it hard to agree on how to run the business—so hard that, in this case, the partners chose to separate.

That's what happens when you don't have a company operating system. An operating system is a structured way to determine what everyone should do and how, and to keep people in line with those decisions over time. Without it, even the smallest teams can quickly fall apart. The more a company's growth accelerates, the more essential the operating system becomes.

Jonathan learned that lesson with the failure of 3D New Media. A few years later, he was building his third startup, Wave Dispersion Technologies, which designed maritime fences. Initially focused on preventing beach erosion, the company pivoted to become an innovative defense system that protected government and sovereign clients against waterborne explosives.

This time, he implemented a company operating system from the start. Again, he engaged Gino Wickman, who by then had founded EOS and written *Traction: Get a Grip on Your Business*. EOS Worldwide had become a robust organization with a concrete methodology and tools that have helped thousands of emerging growth businesses develop scaling infrastructure. Jonathan implemented EOS to keep his team aligned through the challenges of finding a viable market for the business, and it played a critical role in the company's growth from $500,000 to $15 million.

If you want to grow, you *must* have a company operating system. It's what keeps everyone on the same page, working smoothly together toward shared goals. As Expert EOS Implementers, we know EOS does that job beautifully, but it's not the only operating system out there. You're welcome to explore other options, but beware of dabbling. An operating system only works when everyone uses it consistently over time, so you won't see results until you pick one system and fully commit to it.

When you do, you'll see that the power of a company operating system is transformative. A team of average people operating on one system and speaking the same language will reliably outproduce above-average people doing things their own way. In other words, an operating system turns an ordinary team into a high-performing team—and that's exactly what you need to accelerate your growth.

The Six Key Components® of EOS

EOS is such an effective operating system because it provides a comprehensive framework for strengthening the six make-or-break elements of any business.

Vision: Creating clarity around where the company is going and how it will get there. This includes Core Values, Core Focus, and Core Target that unite the organization.

People: Ensuring the right people are in the right seats with clear roles and accountability. This involves hiring for cultural fit and capability while developing team members.

Data: Managing operations with objective information rather than opinions and feelings. This requires identifying key measurables that provide real-time business health indicators that can help navigate toward the desired outcomes.

Issues: Developing systematic approaches to identify, discuss, and solve problems as they arise. This prevents small issues from becoming major obstacles, and it creates decision-making and issue-solving abilities in the organization.

Process: Documenting and following core processes to ensure consistency and efficiency. This creates value beyond individual contributions and ensures that all processes are followed consistently to produce results.

Traction®: Bringing vision to reality through disciplined execution and accountability. This involves setting quarterly priorities, focusing energy in a ninety-day world, and maintaining a meeting pulse.

Even if companies have years of stagnation, EOS can breathe new life into a business. That's what happened at one life sciences firm that struggled repeatedly with vision alignment, accountability, and personnel issues. Like many small to medium businesses, the leadership team had worked hard to grow fast but hadn't developed systems for sustained success. "The company's eleven years old," the Chief Operating Officer said. "We've been through countless folks who haven't done anything with us."

Implementing EOS changed that by getting every member of the executive team on the same page, fully engaged. Previously, each executive had quarterly goals that seemed achievable, but only 50 percent were completed. "After closing our first full quarter using EOS, 70 percent of the goals got accomplished," the COO reported. This improvement didn't come from individual heroics. It came from applying systematic tools. EOS provided structure to enable consistent execution while maintaining team health.

So, let's take a closer look at each of the six elements of EOS. How strong is *your* business in each of these areas?

Vision: Articulate Who You Are

Good business leaders create a vision, articulate the vision, passionately own the vision, and relentlessly drive it to completion. This fundamental truth became crystal clear when we witnessed Ford Motor Company's transformation under Alan Mulally's leadership. When Mulally joined Ford as CEO in September 2006, the company was posting a $5.6 billion quarterly loss. His response? Create the One Ford Vision, specifying how people would work together toward "one team, one plan, one goal."

Mulally's consistent communication of this vision to everyone, everywhere, gave legs to Ford's growth. Joe Nocera noted in *the New York Times* that Mulally "repeated it at the start of every meeting, whether the audience was Ford executives, securities analysts or journalists."[16] The result? Ford transitioned from losing $12.6 billion in 2006 to making $8.6 billion in 2013.

This transformation illustrates a critical principle we've learned through implementing EOS with hundreds of companies: vision drives everything. Without a shared vision grounded in common core values, even the most talented teams struggle to achieve sustained growth.

Vision building starts with core values—the three to seven essential characteristics that define organizational culture. These might include integrity, innovative spirit, or a roll-up-your-sleeves attitude. Once defined, it's crucial to repeat core values consistently and use them as actual standards for decisions and behavior.

When we conduct two-day vision-building sessions, we begin by clarifying core values. Building a culture of people who embrace your vision requires consistent communication of these values. Hire people who share these values, review performance against them, and share stories demonstrating how success stems from living the values.

After vision-building sessions, we assign homework: creating a core values speech. This one-page outline clearly defines what each core value means using stories, analogies, and examples. This enables every leader to communicate values consistently and clearly.

People: Get the Right Fit

A high-growth team isn't just a collection of talented individuals. It's a puzzle where each person has to fit with their specific role within the company's big picture. Piecing this puzzle together is harder than most leaders expect, especially when the company is growing fast.

That's what Joseph Kopser found when he was building RideScout. After serving as a Lieutenant Colonel with a daily Pentagon commute, Kopser wanted tools to determine optimal transportation options based on roadway and transit conditions. He co-founded RideScout with his West Point classmate, Craig Cummings, to develop a mobile app that displays real-time transportation information.

The founding team added two more former officers, creating four accomplished leaders accustomed to commanding 800-soldier battalions. Obviously, these were immensely talented people. However, translating military leadership skills into startup management proved challenging. The military's "I've got your back" foundation sometimes created business barriers.

"Initially, there was too much redundancy in what we were doing," co-founder Craig Cummings explained. "We had two team members operating both operations and business development. It was working but created some confusion."

When working with Joseph and Craig to implement EOS, the initial focus centered on accountability and getting the right people in the right seats. Craig noted, "We realized the need to be very clear with roles and responsibilities both internally and externally. We assigned titles so one person was Vice President of Operations and the other was Vice President of Business Development."

The team found value in assigning weekly to-dos and quarterly Rocks[17] to specific individuals. "People and Rocks go hand in hand," Craig said. "You take ownership of that Rock, and it's on you to accomplish the goal."

This accountability structure helped overcome their tendency for everyone to help each other—a good trait except when it creates overlap or gaps. "I don't have time anymore to help my colleague with his Rock—I'm working on my Rock, and he's working on his," Craig explained. "This especially resonated with our core team of four army veterans. We come from an institution that focuses on accountability, for leaders to take responsibility for their actions. It's nice to have that reinforced."

With clear accountability for the right people in the right seats, RideScout rapidly deployed its service in fifty US cities. By September 2014, Moovel GmbH, a Mercedes-Benz unit, announced it would purchase RideScout. The company's rapid growth stemmed from its ability to focus on both business and individual priorities.

"There are so many things we could be doing," Craig reflected. "But at the end of the day, our EOS Implementer and EOS helped us focus."

This relief comes from using systematic tools to put decisions about people and roles into objective terms. By removing emotion from the equation and focusing on what's best for the organization, the team can avoid the personnel issues that so often drag organizations into dysfunction.

Data: Measure What Matters

Even with a clear shared vision and the right people in the right seats, confusion can arise if everyone doesn't agree on how to measure success.

We saw this in a commercial painting business with 200 field painters, where each job team included a foreman and two painters. Business owners measured growth and profitability through gross margin, which was influenced by three key inputs: labor, materials, and equipment rentals. However, the foremen weren't always aware of this, so they sometimes made choices that unintentionally lowered their gross margin.

In one instance, a foreman ordered three material hoists on Wednesday to finish by a Friday deadline. He thought he was doing the right thing, not realizing he was adversely impacting the job's gross margin. Had the foreman understood the leadership team's success metrics, he could have called the project manager to request schedule adjustments. He could also take other proactive measures to improve gross margin, like teaching painters not to overload brushes, which would reduce material costs per job.

Many organizations understand the value of measurement but don't consistently collect or review the data they need. That's why scorecards (a.k.a. dashboards) are a key feature of EOS. A scorecard lists critical weekly pulse measurements that lead to the company's desired outcomes. These can be actions, behaviors, activities, key drivers, or leading indicators, and each metric has a target and an owner.

This navigation tool puts the right information front and center, not just occasionally but every single week. That keeps each member of the leadership team aligned with what matters, aware of where the business stands, and accountable for producing results. It also helps them identify patterns and trends, flesh out issues, and keep a pulse on their teams.

One of our clients holds Monday morning scorecard reviews with the leadership team. "We have certain things we have to report every week, such as how much we are billing," the COO explained. "Are we meeting our target? How many employees do we have? How many clients were touched this week? We're all more knowledgeable and accountable."

Craig Cummings from RideScout credits the scorecard as "a key instrument for the team." Selecting meaningful measurements is essential. His team asks whether each metric truly helps accomplish company goals. "There's so much to keep track of—the scorecard helps us keep track of the right amount and the right measurables. The scorecards are the key piece for accomplishing our goals."

Issues: Resolve Problems Systematically

When people miss goals, new issues arise while old ones fester, preventing traction and productivity. Many individuals and leadership teams circle around issues without resolution. Learning to resolve and move beyond issues is essential for organizational health and growth.

There are many issue-solving and decision-making methodologies. The EOS system uses IDS® (Identify, Discuss, Solve) for tackling issues quickly and efficiently. First, the leadership team compiles a list of issues from all members. Then, they prioritize that list together. Finally, one issue at a time, they go through the following three steps:

- **Identify:** Get clear on the real root issue
- **Discuss:** Talk through it objectively and briefly
- **Solve:** Determine the next step, to-do, or decision

For example, one client experiencing extremely fast growth faced challenges with their Chinese manufacturing partner, who sent 50 percent more product than ordered. The manufacturer demanded payment, despite contracts allowing only a ±10 percent variance. Here's how they used IDS in this situation:

Identify: The client received excess product that they couldn't store cost-effectively, with the vendor demanding payment for non-contracted variance.

Discuss: They explored whether this represented a core values conflict. It was more of a practical problem involving differences in language, culture, and business.

Solve: They determined the vendor's motivation to see if interests could align. The manufacturer found it easier to run full production and felt pressure from investors to maximize profits. To align incentives, they implemented third-party inspections, creating disincentives for overruns—excess product would return to the manufacturer.

Process: Produce Consistent Results

You spend most of your time working "in" your business, delivering products or services. Working "on" your business involves activities that make it resilient, stable, and valuable. Taking time to work "on" your business helps gain control and increase valuation.

The more time spent working "on" your business, the easier it becomes to distinguish, simplify, document, and implement core processes. Eventually, you'll see that core processes are your business—the framework making economics work. This is your "secret sauce" for consistent results.

It can be helpful to divide your processes into "front stage" and "back stage," a concept called The Front Stage/Back Stage Model®, introduced by Dan Sullivan from Strategic Coach®. The Strategic Coach organization was intentionally designed around producing excellent "front stage" shows through well-documented "back stage" processes.

For example, consider a Bavarian restaurant renowned for its lively biergarten experiences and homemade sausage aromas. That's "front stage." Customers don't want to know how sausage is made—that would ruin the experience. But your team needs to know the sausage-making process. That's "back stage."

Front stage processes represent client-facing activities, including marketing, sales, and service delivery. This is what clients experience.

We like to call them "proven" processes because they demonstrate to prospects that you have a proven way of getting results. You should be able to show your proven process as a one-page visual illustration of how your organization serves customers. As part of your marketing strategy, it builds trust with prospects and helps sales teams create consistent expectations.

For example, BPP Wealth's proven process is the Security Income Planner™. The founder, Debra Schatzki, developed it in collaboration with her coach and further evolved it through the EOS implementation process. "What's been so amazing," she said, "is that the build out of our process also includes the build out of our company: what our core focus is, what that means, what it does, and who we serve."

Back stage—what we call "core"—processes comprise administrative, operational, and support processes that help deliver the front stage experience. This happens behind closed doors.

Every business has core processes—essential activities done consistently well regardless of who performs them. Most companies have HR or people processes, marketing processes, sales processes, operations processes, accounting processes, and customer service processes. Once your team agrees on core processes and names them permanently, you must document them in detail, train employees, and measure compliance until they're "followed by all."

Effective process playbooks have additional elements:

- Document the high-level, secret sauce playbook—the 20 percent that gets 80 percent of the results consistently

- Process names that reflect outcomes or activities (e.g., "How to Hire and Onboard the Right Person in the Right Seat" vs. "HR Process")

- Checklist format so that action is prompted—"bullet points get read, checkboxes get checked"

- One to five pages of actions with references to supporting SOPs and policies

A process-centric organization is the opposite of a hero-centric organization. Hero-centric organizations run on leadership, drive, and ambition but lack operating systems for sustainable growth. As a result, the team ends up operating like young children playing soccer, herding chaotically around the ball and occasionally scoring through happy accidents.

By contrast, process-centric organizations align vision and drive traction through documented ways of working. They improve performance, adapt to change, and effectively manage competitive pressures. This transforms a "herd ball" team into a professional, organized group that delivers consistent, predictable, scalable results.

Traction: Prioritize Your Actions

When Ford CEO Alan Mulally stepped down in July 2014, COO Mark Fields succeeded him. Fields helped institute the One Ford vision and played an important role in helping the company gain traction. Traction for Ford meant weekly business plan review meetings, tracking the One Ford plan's progress, and monitoring global business environments. Fields led Thursday meetings that were credited with driving reliable and transparent processes for running Ford's global operations, enabling senior leadership to collaborate and take decisive action.

In EOS, we define priorities and create traction using SMART Rocks (Specific, Measurable, Attainable, Realistic, Timely). Rocks are the three to seven crucial tasks or goals that need to be accomplished in the next ninety days. The term Rocks comes from the popular parable of fitting rocks, pebbles, and sand into a jar. If you start with the sand and pebbles—the smaller, less important tasks—you won't have room for the rocks. But if you put the rocks in first, you can fit the pebbles around them and the sand around the pebbles.

Rocks force the leadership team to break down overwhelming annual goals into achievable "90-Day Worlds", creating more manageable quarterly goals. That keeps them focused on what's most important and clears away distractions. This increased intensity helps leaders gain meaningful, measurable traction.

When companies like RideScout move fast to build markets, they risk choking on too many priorities. Co-Founder Craig Cummings said developing Rocks worked especially well for their team. The concept focuses companies, leadership teams, and employees on vision through specific, documented quarterly and weekly goals.

"It was easily understood that we would say this is our Rock for the fourth quarter and always check to see if we accomplished those Rocks," Craig explained. "It sets a tight, clean goal for individuals, provides accountability, and lets everyone know what everyone's working on."

EOS Brings Freedom of Time

Dave Chronister, founder and Managing Partner of Parameter Security, is proof that with the right systems and support, even the most demanding businesses can thrive—and their leaders can finally reclaim their time. As one of the nation's leading cybersecurity experts, Dave built Parameter Security into a trusted name for penetration testing, incident response, and computer forensics, serving highly regulated industries like finance and healthcare. But for years, the business demanded his constant attention, leaving little room for rest or personal freedom.

That changed when Dave implemented the Entrepreneurial Operating System. With EOS, Dave and his leadership team established clear processes, accountability, and a culture of discipline, allowing the company to run smoothly—even in his absence. For the first time since founding Parameter Security, Dave was able to take a real vacation without worrying about the day-to-day operations. The business not only survived but continued to thrive, proving that true freedom for a founder comes from building a self-managing company.

Beyond his technical expertise, Dave is a sought-after commentator on cybersecurity systems, policies, and best practices, regularly appearing on national outlets like CNN, CNBC, and Fox Business. As a member of the Entrepreneurs' Organization (EO), he continues to invest in his own growth and network, leveraging peer insights to keep Parameter Security at the forefront of the industry. Dave has achieved what many founders only dream of: a business that grows, innovates, and protects clients—while giving its leader the freedom to truly live.

Implementing Your Company Operating System

"Having" a company operating system means nothing unless you use it, and the most important use of it happens in one place: leadership team meetings. The Meeting Pulse® prescribes that leadership teams meet weekly for ninety minutes, quarterly for full days, and annually for two days. This enables teams to stay focused and aligned, solving problems and preventing the burnout and exhaustion that come with firefighting becoming a daily job.

Initially, clients resist more meetings. By implementing the right meetings in the right meeting pulse, leadership teams—and eventually departments—conduct meetings that accomplish more rather than waste time. Most people procrastinate naturally. If leadership holds quarterly sessions, they'll be able to accomplish goals in between. When you also meet weekly, you can get even more done.

When Debra Schatzki's broker gave BPP Wealth one month to become a registered investment advisory company, she credits EOS Rocks and weekly meetings with achieving the goal. "We had to get it all up and running, transfer clients, set up operation and billing systems, and establish our ability to service clients—better than before," she said.

What seemed impossible became specific, measurable goals with accountability. "The result is that we got it up and running and billed 25 percent more because of the transfer," Debra said. "Because we had to get paperwork, clients gave us more business. After running for a year, we doubled the income."

RideScout's rapid transformation from a startup to a scaled business acquired by a major global transportation player demonstrates the power of systematic implementation. Joseph and Craig focused early on building accountability and establishing Rocks. Their ability to expand across cities stemmed from discipline and execution. That's true traction.

Chapter Takeaways

- Implementing an operating system provides one piece for optimizing business growth.

- EOS is an extremely effective operating system because it provides a comprehensive framework for strengthening the six make-or-break elements of any business: vision, people, data, issues, process, and traction.

- Implementation of a company operating system happens primarily in leadership meetings and requires full buy-in from the entire leadership team.

- You must choose one operating system for your company; you can't run on multiple.

[3]

OPTIMIZE YOUR COMMUNITY: THE POWER OF PEER ADVISORY AND SUPPORT

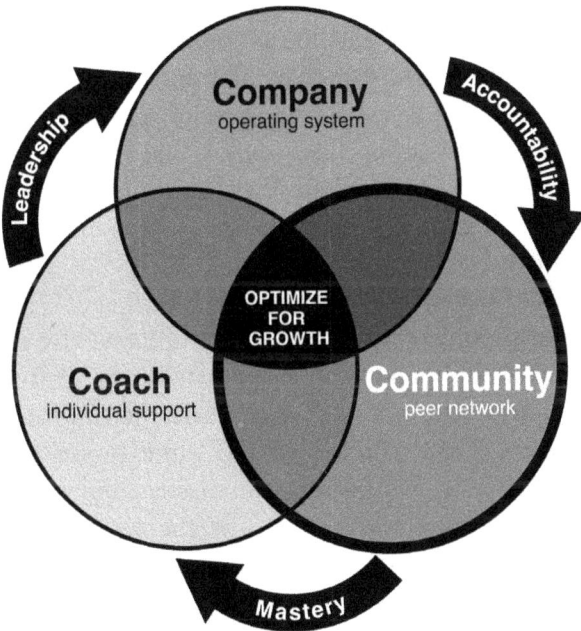

Years ago, at Jonathan's former company, Wave Dispersion Technologies, Inc., a client refused to pay a $50,000 invoice after its company went bankrupt. That was a major financial blow to the young company—they had been counting on that money to cover their own bills. The Wave Dispersion team wanted payment, plus controls to prevent similar situations.

Jonathan wasn't sure how to handle the situation, but thankfully, he didn't have to figure it out by himself. He was a member of an Entrepreneurs' Organization (EO) Forum—a confidential, peer-sharing program with owners of similar-sized businesses from non-competitive industries. Surely someone in the group had faced a similar situation and would have a good solution.

So, Jonathan shared the problem with his EO Forum group. One member suggested always filing UCC-1 Statements—mortgage instruments securing vendor claims to assigned collateral—for sales of $50,000 or more, where counterparty credit was a concern. Jonathan and his team immediately implemented this process for future sales, and they never had to worry about losing big client payments again.

This peer input catapulted Jonathan up the typical entrepreneur learning curve—he took the elevator instead of the stairs.

As Isaac Newton said, "If I have seen further, it is by standing on the shoulders of giants." This captures why even the most capable entrepreneurial leaders need peer advisory support. Trial and error is costly; why waste the time and effort when someone else has solved the same problem before? Collective experience is a shortcut to mastery and growth.

That's why a peer community is the second leg of the Optimize for Growth Model. No matter the size of the business, an entrepreneur alone is an entrepreneur at risk—at risk of making unnecessary mistakes, wasting resources, and stalling out. By regularly engaging with other business leaders, you can leverage their collective wisdom to discover new ideas, different perspectives, helpful solutions, and tools to accelerate your business.

The Power of Multiple Heads

Research has shown that peer advisory groups have a measurable impact on business results. According to one study by *Chief Executive*, peer network members grew more than twice as fast and were twice as profitable as their industry average.[18] Another study found that peer group participants consistently report real financial gains—often in the millions of dollars—as a direct result of skills learned, decisions made, or opportunities found in their group.[19] Those are significant financial benefits.

However, the power of peer advisory extends beyond business metrics. For entrepreneurs facing the isolation of leadership, peer groups provide essential emotional and psychological support. Research suggests that peer support significantly improves leaders' mental health and decision-making confidence. And it's becoming more and more common: recent research by McKinsey identified "harnessing the power of peer networks" as one of the top four ways CEO leadership is shifting in response to global challenges.[20]

From what the research shows and what we've seen in practice with our clients, there are six key benefits of participating in a peer community.

Accelerating Your Learning: Regularly connecting with other leaders in similar positions allows you to learn from their experiences. You can avoid their mistakes and borrow their solutions without having to figure it all out on your own, shortening your path to mastery of your role.

Anticipating Potential Issues: Instead of waiting for problems to arise, you can prevent them proactively by paying attention to the problems your peers experience. You'll learn

JONATHAN B. SMITH AND JEANET L. WADE

to notice red flags earlier and take quick action before a small issue turns into a major catastrophe.

Testing Decisions: When you're contemplating making a bold move, you can put it in front of your peer group and see how they respond. They may point out risks or possibilities you hadn't considered, allowing you to make a more thoughtful decision than if you had proceeded without external feedback.

Calibrating Your Perspective: When you're isolated, every problem can seem like a disaster. In a peer group, it's easier to distinguish between minor setbacks every company goes through and the truly serious problems that can threaten the survival of the business.

Sparking New Ideas: When you're building a new company, often you don't know what you don't know. Other business leaders might show you possibilities, tools, and solutions you never considered before.

Holding You Accountable: A company operating system creates accountability, as does a coach (more on that in the next chapter), but a peer group provides that extra spark of inspiration and motivation. They'll push you to set higher goals for yourself and your business, and they won't let you forget what you set out to do.

These benefits create a very real return on your investment of time and money. When members calculate the value of speakers, issue processing sessions, peak performers, network access, coaching, and learning experiences, the ROI is undeniable.

It's worth noting that these benefits only come from committed, consistent engagement with the group. At first, some executives feel skeptical about participating in a peer group. They worry about sharing too much information or being judged by others, so they hold back. But they soon learn that everyone is in the same boat, no one has all the answers, and you can't get the help you need unless you speak up.

As Doug Davidoff, founder of Imagine Business Development, put it: "I learned that successful business owners had as much uncertainty as I had. There was no magic answer . . . At the end of the day, I want to know if I'm asking the right question. A peer group lets you find that space where you've thought it through enough. It allows you to make faster decisions with more confidence."

Peer Communities in Action

Until you start participating regularly in a peer community, it's hard to imagine exactly what it will do for you and your business. Here are five real stories from our clients to give you an idea of what you stand to gain.

Reversing a Downward Trend

A manufacturing CEO facing declining sales and operational inefficiencies presented his challenges to his peer advisory group. The group provided valuable insights, suggesting concrete ways to streamline operations and diversify the product line. With the group leader's support, the CEO implemented these new strategies, simultaneously cutting costs and growing revenues. The company not only reversed its downward trend but soon achieved record profitability.

Easing the Growing Pains

The leader of a fast-growing tech startup was struggling with leadership transitions and maintaining company culture during rapid expansion. Unsurprisingly, several other leaders in his peer group had experienced the same challenges. They shared what they learned about planning succession, structuring a growing organization, and supporting team morale through periods of rapid change. Their diverse perspectives enabled the CEO to make more informed decisions about handling leadership changes and team growth, resulting in smoother transitions and a stronger company culture.

Testing a Strategic Pivot

After two years, the CEO of a business development firm wanted to make a bold strategic move. Before he pulled the trigger, he presented the idea to his peer community. Most of them considered it risky, and they brought up a number of legitimate concerns. However, through the process of discussing those potential issues, the CEO realized he had thought it through as much as possible and taken every measure to mitigate the risks. He knew it was time to implement the change, and within two weeks, the company had its first client for its new services.

Upgrading the Team

A young man took over the family business just as it was starting to grow, and it soon became clear that the team would have to evolve with the company. Most of the team were friends who had been there since the early days, and some of them were no longer the right fit for their roles. The most challenging issue arose when the CEO realized that his COO was a good doer but not a strategic thinker. He brought this issue to his peer group, and his fellow business leaders helped him plan a transition to a more capable COO who could execute the company's vision. This started a chain reaction of more strategic hires; as profits increased, higher-quality personnel could be added to the team. In time, the CEO was able to step back from daily operations and trust his team to execute.

Building Internal Trust

The CEO of an industrial materials reclamation company often felt frustrated with his sales leader when sales fell short of expectations. This was the biggest source of worry for the CEO, and the conflict created tension on the executive team. So, the CEO brought the issue to his peer group for feedback.

A sales leader at another company in the group talked him off the ledge, sharing insights about the challenges of sales and encouraging patience. The CEO accepted the need to "stay in his operations lane" and had a conversation with the sales leader, sharing the perspective he received from his group. It helped the two build trust in each other and in the EOS Model®, and in time, sales rose to meet and surpass the company's targets.

Optimized for Exit

Tracy and Brad Butler, brothers and co-founders of Acropolis Technology Group, built one of St. Louis's most respected managed IT service providers from the ground up. Launching Acropolis in 1996, they combined Tracy's leadership and Brad's technical expertise to create a company known for its disciplined operations, dedicated service teams, and a culture that consistently earned "Best of Business" accolades. Over nearly three decades, the Butlers navigated the fast-changing technology landscape, always prioritizing both client success and employee well-being.

When the time came to consider their exit, Tracy and Brad leveraged their long-standing involvement in an industry peer group and the fact that they ran their business on EOS to prepare the business for sale. Their commitment to building a process-driven, customer-centric organization paid off: in 2023, Acropolis was acquired by a leading national MSP at a strong multiple on business value. The brothers ensured their employees were set up for long-term success, negotiating terms that preserved jobs and provided new growth opportunities within a larger organization. This thoughtful transition reflected their belief that a business's legacy is measured not just by financial results, but by the opportunities it creates for its people.

The Butlers credit much of their success to the power of community and continuous improvement that came from EOS and their industry group. Their peer group experience provided invaluable insights, accountability, and support throughout the journey—from scaling up to navigating industry shifts to planning a successful exit. EOS provided the framework for clear vision alignment, accountability, and a healthy culture. Tracy and Brad's story stands as a testament to the impact of disciplined leadership, peer collaboration, and a people-first approach in building—and successfully transitioning—a thriving business. In fact, Tracy was so impressed with the impact of this approach that, after exiting the business, he trained to become a Professional EOS Implementer® and help other entrepreneurs grow.

Peer Group Criteria

To ensure a positive and productive experience with your peer community, it's important to choose a group that's a good fit for you. Here are ten characteristics to look for.

1. **Similar Company Size:** A $2 million business owner cannot relate to $50 million owners but will learn from $15 million owners.

2. **Similar Authority Level:** Other members should have responsibilities and decision-making powers at the same level as you—running businesses with the final say on strategic direction, employee issues, and other crucial decisions.

3. **Similar Goals:** Some groups focus solely on professional development and business growth, while others also address issues like family, work-life balance, and personal growth. This may not be apparent initially, but group dynamics will reflect members' goals, and you'll thrive best with peers whose goals are similar to yours.

4. **Non-Competitive:** To promote a supportive and open environment for all participants, the organizers should ensure that direct competitors are not in the same peer group.

5. **Confidential:** What's shared in the group must stay in the group. This creates the psychological safety that's essential for an open and productive group dynamic.

6. **Committed:** When everyone commits wholeheartedly to the group's principles, format, and ideals, the experience is more fulfilling for all.

7. **Diverse:** Groups with varied backgrounds, industries, and experience levels provide richer perspectives.

8. **Honest:** Trust develops when members share real challenges rather than maintaining facades.

9. **Engaged:** Consistent attendance and engagement are essential for building relationships and momentum.

10. **Professionally Facilitated:** Skilled facilitators keep discussions productive and ensure all voices are heard.

Some leaders remain in the same peer group for many years; longevity benefits the trust and relationships developed over time. Others outgrow their groups and migrate to new ones, matching business changes, life stages, and personal goals. Eventually, you may develop networking skills and relationships to form ad hoc peer groups. You'll entrust select experts and advisors to be your sounding board for key decisions and issues. However you choose to build your community of peers, it's essential to continuously leverage their feedback to accelerate your business growth.

Where High-Growth Founders Find Their People

Peer communities for business leaders have been around for decades. And yet, Sam Parr and Joe Speiser felt something was missing. As they had experienced firsthand, the challenges of running a high-growth, tech-focused startup were simply not the same as what other business owners faced. Peers who faced similar situations were few and far between, especially outside of startup-heavy areas like Silicon Valley and New York City. It was hard to find a safe space to share knowledge and emotional support.

So in 2023, they created Hampton. Unlike other peer group organizations, Hampton focuses exclusively on fast-growing startups that leverage technology. Their members have reached at least $3 million in annual revenue or capital raised, or they've sold a startup for at least $10 million. Plus, each member goes through a thorough vetting and interview process to ensure they're a good fit for the community.

The core membership experience revolves around groups of eight founders, led by professional facilitators. The groups are intentionally designed to mix founders in different industries and at different stages of business and life. That brings diverse perspectives to every conversation and creates a balance of mentors, mentees, and mirrors in each group. In addition to the monthly groups, membership includes a highly active online community, in-person events, guest speakers, exclusive discounts, and other perks.

Perhaps the most important quality of Hampton is that it's strictly confidential. Members can openly talk about sensitive topics, like raising capital, negotiating exits, solving employee problems, and even managing family and personal issues. They can get genuine support and answers from people who have been in the same boat—something they can't find anywhere else.

Where to Find a Peer Group

Chances are that one of several peer network organizations has local membership near you. Peer advisory groups come in various shapes and sizes. Some are formal with membership dues, bylaws, and strict criteria in exchange for the predictability and baked-in trust among the members. Others are free with loose principles and easy entry.

You can likely find a peer group regardless of location through Chambers of Commerce, houses of worship, or Internet searches. The optimization comes from finding the right community to support your business type and issues. This could be a formal peer advisory group, networking at an industry association, or joining a cohort of people working on a specific topic (i.e., AI).

The following are some examples of peer advisory groups. This is by no means a comprehensive list. Be sure to search in your local area for groups near you. Also, consider different types of communities that will give you the perspective and support you want.

The Alternative Board (TAB) targets local small and medium business owners in non-competing businesses with five to ten members. Each board is formed and facilitated by a Certified Business Coach or Facilitator, meeting monthly. Members may also meet with facilitators for private coaching.

Entrepreneurs' Organization focuses on entrepreneurs with member-led groups. EO provides executive education, mentorships, and global events. Their philosophy centers on "gestalt protocol" and sharing individual experience rather than giving advice. The magic lies in realizing that other members often have expertise around issues you're facing.

Hampton is an exclusive membership community for founders and CEOs of high-growth, tech-focused startups. Its core purpose centers on cultivating a founder-focused peer network, with a primary emphasis on core groups of peers, executive facilitators, ongoing knowledge sharing among peers, and incredible in-person events.

Renaissance Executive Forums is an international peer group organization for CEOs, Presidents, and Owners. Renaissance brings top executives from non-competing, similar-sized companies into peer advisory forums. Members participate in monthly meetings, quarterly coaching, and annual learning retreats. Each Forum is facilitated by trained, experienced Forum Leaders.

Vistage is known for its CEO and small business forums, which feature up to sixteen members from similar-sized companies across various industries. An experienced Vistage Chair facilitates monthly full-day meetings. Members receive monthly private executive coaching from the Chair. The global organization also provides groups for key executive development.

Women Presidents Organization (WPO) is a nonprofit for women presidents of multimillion-dollar companies. Professionally facilitated peer group meetings help female leaders achieve success as women and for their organizations.

Young Presidents' Organization (YPO) is the global networking organization for company leaders under forty-five. YPO hosts forums, events, mentoring programs, and learning events across 125 countries. YPO's prestige provides access to corporate and government leaders, plus active social communities. YPO emphasizes "whole person" development and personal and professional fulfillment.

NOTE: The above organizations focus on executive leadership across geographies and industries. However, you may also benefit from a peer group that is specific to your local area or industry. See the Resources section at the end of this book for more community and peer advisory group options.

Chapter Takeaways

- As businesses scale, the challenges become increasingly complex and the stakes higher, and having access to collective wisdom from a community of business leaders becomes invaluable.

- The right community of peers provides six key benefits: accelerating your learning, anticipating potential issues, testing decisions, calibrating your perspective, sparking new ideas, and holding you accountable.

- The key is selecting the right group for your circumstances and goals and participating fully on a regular basis.

- Community peer groups come in various types: formal and organized peer organizations, industry trade associations, informal community peer groups, and many others.

[4]

OPTIMIZE YOU: THE IMPACT OF EXECUTIVE COACHING

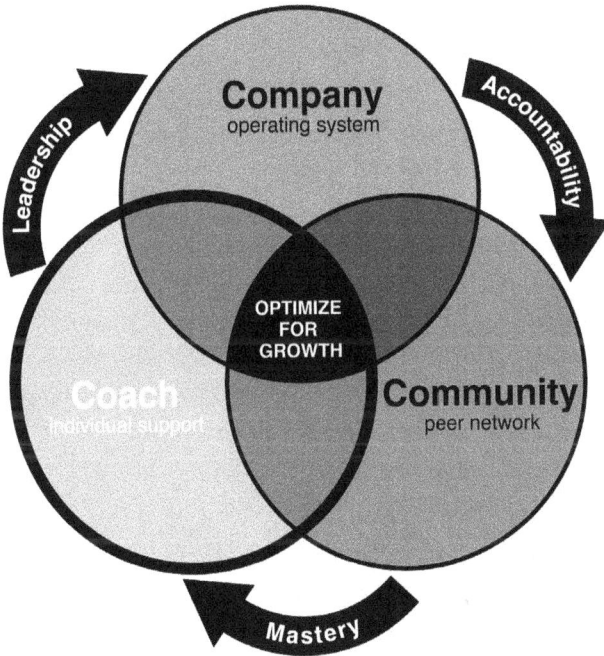

When Erica Marrari was promoted to VP of Client Services at 5AM Solutions, she knew she would need guidance. It was her first executive role, and as a woman in the male-dominated science and technology landscape, she wanted to cultivate an approach that worked for her context. "I wanted assistance with managing the role," she said. "I realized my success would have more to do with leadership style than anything else."

So, Erica hired a coach. She looked for someone who could relate to her circumstances and had achieved the kind of success she envisioned. She found Cindy Morgan, a former VP of Organizational Development and Learning at NYU Langone Medical Center, who was then in the same role at Penn Medicine. Cindy had many years under her belt as an executive in science and technology organizations, and she could help Erica navigate her new leadership role.

One of the first things they worked on was learning to avoid and manage conflicts. "A lot of it centers around language," Erica noted. "I'm a direct person, and Cindy would coach me on how to use alternative language for more of a soft landing. It was about changing the way that I phrased things, asking more questions, and being more analytical." Cindy role-played with Erica so she could learn and practice new approaches to communication. "I've had a lot of people give me guidance, but never in that way," Erica said. "It was a game-changer."

It's not just new executives like Erica who need support. As Eric Schmidt—former CEO and Executive Chairman of Google—put it, "Everybody needs a coach."[21]

It Can Be Lonely at the Top

If there's anything business leaders know, it's that it gets lonely at the top. We even have a little romance around it: the diligent, determined, driven entrepreneur working insane hours with no one who understands their passion or their pain. But having people who understand your passion and your pain won't alleviate the loneliness for very long. To do that, you need meaningful relationships with people who have walked your path.

In Dixie Gillaspie's thirty-plus years of coaching thought leaders and entrepreneurs, she's consistently heard how the world feels lighter on their shoulders just because she gets them, sees them, and has been there before them. Clients who participate in the Super Creator Unlimited groups or are members of one of her Business Creator Circles often tell her that the coaching and community augment each other to not only build clarity, perspective, and momentum, but to evaporate that feeling of being alone.

Recently, a client shared an observation about *why* the community was so empowering for her. She and her best friend have been colleagues, collaborators, and even competitors for years, and they have participated in multiple masterminds and peer groups together. But when they joined forces to start a new business, they started coaching with Dixie and participating in one of her Circles.

"It's the shared language that makes it so easy to know you're in the right place," she said. "Everyone is using the same systems and definitions. And since we speak the same business language, it's easier to connect, learn, communicate, and support each other."

It's so true, if you're in a group of leaders who run their business on EOS, you know exactly what they mean when they use words like "Traction," "Level 10 Meeting®," and "Rocks." If you're in a group of people who are using the Super Creator Vision 2 Reality method, you know exactly what they mean when they say "creative tension," "super creator orientation," and "staying in the end result."

And this is where the power of a company operating system, a personal coach, and an aligned community really serves you at the highest level—when you not only share experiences and knowledge but also a common structure and language.

Peer communities alone can be helpful, but in a group setting, you can't always find the expertise or get the individual support you need. Plus, the challenges you face will grow along with your business, and your personal leadership capabilities have to keep up.

That's why every business leader needs a coach. A coach may be the only person who can give you honest feedback, problem-solve with you, and hold you accountable to your professional and personal goals. If you've made it this far in your business, you clearly have some management skills, but if you want to become a high-growth, high-impact leader, you'll need the support and wisdom of a trusted advisor.

The ROI of Coaching

Coaching is increasingly being adopted by professionals and organizations worldwide, and that's because *it works*.

From a financial standpoint, multiple studies have shown that executive coaching reliably pays back what you put into it. One study found a median ROI of 700 percent, with 86 percent of organizations seeing positive returns.[22] Another found an average return of 221 percent, with some businesses reporting returns of up to fifty times their coaching investment.[23]

From a skill development perspective, coaching is the most effective way to accelerate learning. A comprehensive meta-analysis of executive coaching studies found that coaching has the strongest impact on behavioral outcomes, especially cognitive behavioral activities.[24] The study showed significant positive effects for self-efficacy, psychological capital, and resilience—outcomes considered relatively stable over time.

Both individual leaders and their organizations benefit from executive coaching.

For example:

- 80 percent of coaching clients report improved self-confidence and self-awareness, leading to better decision-making[25]
- 70 percent see notable improvements in work performance, relationships, and communication skills[26]
- 51 percent of companies with strong coaching cultures report higher revenue growth than industry peers[27]
- Companies investing in executive coaching experience, on average, a 48 percent improvement in organizational effectiveness[28]

The ROI is undeniable, but if you've never worked with a coach before, you might be wondering where it comes from. What exactly does an executive coach *do?*

What Coaches Do

Essentially, an executive coach does the same thing any kind of coach does: push you to fulfill your full potential. They help you clarify your goals, build on your strengths, shore up your weaknesses, overcome obstacles, stay motivated, and course correct when you get off track.

It's not so different from what a sports coach does for an athlete, except that in this case, the sport is growing your company. They will help you develop and use the key skills for the business leadership arena, shaping your approach to your organization and the people in it. Most importantly, they are the person you can go to when you're struggling or unsure. With your coach, you can be totally honest and get the support you need, without worrying about losing face or undermining your authority.

Lieutenant General (Ret.) David Huntoon Jr., who led training of military officers at West Point and now heads D2H Consulting, put it this way: "Coaching and mentoring are continuous requirements in any organization that values growth, adapting to the extraordinary change we see in the marketplace today." David noted that the military values and reinforces leadership development through continuous cycles of training, development, coaching, and mentorship from day one.

"Coaching and mentoring are very effective reinforcing techniques in leader development," he said. "The opportunity to take a complex leadership concern to a trusted superior allows you to lay out your issue in complete candor and gain the wisdom of greater experience without being judged."

Alicia Marie, founder of the coaching and training organization People Biz, noted that the biggest challenge is always people: "You can have systems in place, but what people underestimate is that people are the levers. I've seen people with all sorts of resources fail because they weren't paying attention to the people. Anyone can be successful on their own. But can you help another person reach their optimum level? That takes skill. Until leaders and managers can do that, they're at a disadvantage. Companies that do that will have a huge advantage. That's where coaching comes in."

One of the most valuable things a coach can do is reduce the chaos and overwhelm in your life. As Mark Huge, executive coach and founder of Work Flow Facilitators, told us, "There's always more to be done than can be done. When people get overwhelmed, they need a system." Fourteen years ago, Mark saw this at the Cleveland Clinic, where he volunteered, helping patients in treatment to resolve personal and professional issues. "We would talk about an issue, and the next week, they would still have the same problem. They needed structure to hold them accountable for solving those problems." So, Mark and the doctor he worked with developed what they call the OCE system (Order, Control, Execute) to help people get organized and in control of their tasks, goals, and issues.

Business leaders are just like those patients—they, too, need structure and accountability to get things done. Top leaders, just like top athletes, recognize that a coach will do that much more effectively than they can do it themselves. As Mark emphasizes, being successful doesn't negate the need for a coach. "Mike Phelps has a coach with him virtually all the time—he's with him in the pool," he commented. "Why does Phelps need a coach, being as good as he is?" To help him focus and do what needs to be done, even when it's hard.

That's why the best business leaders work with executive coaches. As we mentioned earlier, Google's Eric Schmidt is a strong proponent of coaching. Alan Mulally, former CEO of Ford and Boeing, worked with the renowned executive coach Marshall Goldsmith, as did Jeff Bezos. Many other top CEOs, including Howard Schultz (Starbucks), Meg Whitman (eBay), and Indra Nooyi (PepsiCo), have all spoken about working with coaches. Today, most top executives have coaches, and large institutions typically have senior organizational development roles—people who work with executive teams to develop leadership skills and resolve issues.

For senior leaders at emerging companies, a coach is especially important because there are fewer people to talk to about struggles on the path to scaling up. "Good coaches ask great questions at the right time," said Cindy Morgan. "And slow you down before you take action that may or may not help you in the long run."

A Coach Turns Chaos Into Systems

In the midst of its rapid disruption to the credit-card payments market, Square—co-founded by Jim McKelvey and Jack Dorsey—faced an existential threat: Amazon had entered the payments space. Despite Square's early success and new market creation, the arrival of this tech giant created great uncertainty and tension. And yet, somehow, Square stood their ground and won the battle.

Jim McKelvey wanted to share this story, not just as a cautionary tale but as a blueprint for entrepreneurial resilience and innovation. He tried to write it on his own, but after several drafts, he realized he needed help—a system, a coach, someone to give him truthful feedback.

So, he called on Amy Scharff, President and Moderator of Leadership Council (née Presidents Council). She had deep roots in the world of C-suite peer advisory and coaching; her father, Arthur Scharff, was one of the early co-creators of proven peer advisory models that support CEOs and entrepreneurs. Amy carried that legacy, guiding leaders through structured, transformative processes that fostered both business and personal growth, enabling them to become better individuals.

Amy's background in the dynamics of group systems, leadership development, the English language, and coaching made her uniquely suited to guide Jim through the process of writing his book. She didn't just act as an editor; she became his writing coach, applying a systematic framework to help Jim:

- Clarify his message and distill complex experiences into deep lessons for other entrepreneurs, dreamers, businesspeople, creators, and business owners alike.

- Structure the narrative so that it could serve as both a memoir and an informative book for businesspeople and inventors.

- Stay accountable to the project through regular collaboration, honest feedback, and milestone celebrations.

Amy's approach was methodical, employing solid coaching practices she had learned as a peer-group moderator, a writing specialist, and a teacher. She worked with Jim and the editors to ensure that each draft was stronger than the last. She advocated for Jim's goals while helping the book retain the high standards the entire team expected.

She also helped assemble that high-performing team—including editors, designers, and PR professionals—to bring the book to life. This collaborative, experimental, self-checking, and iterative approach mirrored the very principles that Square used to differentiate and survive in a turbulent new market.

The result was *The Innovation Stack*, a great read that not only chronicles Square's journey but also provides a series of recognizable steps and stories for would-be inventors and entrepreneurs. Amy's coaching helped Jim shift his writing from some fun stories, cobbled together loosely with little impact, into a strong piece of nonfiction from which businesspeople and dreamers both can draw wisdom and inspiration. The book's successful release—despite launching at the onset of the COVID-19 pandemic—stands as a testament to the power of assertive coaching from within several strong disciplines.

Amy Scharff's collaboration with Jim McKelvey illustrates how transformative a deep knowledge of a few key disciplines can be when used as a framework for coaching.

Through expertise, accountability, and finely tuned facilitation, Amy helped turn Jim's moment of bewilderment when Square "won" against Amazon into a lasting contribution to the entrepreneurial community. Their work exemplifies how a coach, when paired with the appropriate process, can help leaders not only survive change but use it as a springboard for innovation, growth, and mastery.

When to Engage a Coach

According to Cindy Morgan, coaching tends to become a priority for business leaders at certain key moments:

- Taking on a new role (e.g., going from peer to boss)
- Entering a strong culture from the outside
- Being a senior leader (e.g., the executive team)

"When you have people that rise up in the organization," she said, "it's hard to find the right course to teach them the specifics of what to know. It needs to be specific to the person's context. If you can accelerate by increasing your self-awareness during a time of transition, you can exponentially grow and enter jobs and business relationships more intentionally."

Alicia Marie said the number one reason people decide to engage a coach is that they have hit a personal development ceiling. A moment occurs when they're stuck, and they realize they must change to be successful. "That can happen because your entire team of twelve just walked out on you, or you just sold $1 million in product and can't fund it," Marie said. "It can be due to major success or major issues." Either way, the person acknowledges they will have to grow to deal with the circumstance.

However, you don't have to wait to hit a ceiling before you hire a coach. Instead, you can do it proactively as part of your decision to implement the Optimize for Growth system. Your desire to scale up drove you to read this book, and a coach will put you on the most efficient, effective path to do that. Why wait until you hit a roadblock when you can start accelerating now?

Choosing a Coach

Before you work with a coach, it's crucial to be sure you're ready and willing to take their feedback and advice. Are you open to asking frank questions of yourself? Will you experiment with new approaches to working with colleagues and staff? Are you willing to be held accountable to reach your goals?

If the answer is yes, it's time to start your search. The right coach depends on your unique hurdles and current business priorities, but regardless of your circumstances, a good coaching relationship:

- Opens your mind to possibilities and fosters the mindset to succeed
- Provides an objective sounding board
- Shines light on things you struggle to see clearly
- Holds you accountable to your goals
- Brings experience—the coach has been in your shoes before
- Helps you create a legacy—thinks bigger than you do

Coaches vary widely in style and skill, and choosing one takes forethought and due diligence. Begin by asking your mentors and extended network for recommendations based on criteria you've developed (e.g., gender, background, focus). You can narrow your search by asking yourself what skills or issues are the highest priority for you, since executive coaches often specialize in particular areas:

- **Leadership Development:** Enhancing general leadership skills and capabilities

- **Executive Presence:** Developing communication, influence, and gravitas

- **Strategic Thinking:** Improving vision, planning, and decision-making

- **Emotional Intelligence:** Managing self-awareness and relationships

- **Succession Planning:** Developing the next generation of leaders

- **Work-Life Integration:** Balance and personal effectiveness

Interview each candidate to gauge your comfort level, chemistry, and dialogue quality. Cindy Morgan suggests asking yourself basic questions, like, *Can I be my worst self with this person?* "This isn't about pleasing and putting your best face on. It's about being real," she said. For her part, she gauges readiness and fit in part by asking potential clients, "Why coaching, and why now?"

The most effective coaching relationships align the coach's expertise with your specific development needs and business challenges. Research shows that coaching effectiveness increases significantly when there's strong chemistry between coach and client, clear goal-setting processes, and regular progress measurement.

You may find that you need different coaches at different times. What you need to grow today might not be what you need in a few years. It's perfectly fine to switch coaches or even have multiple coaches for different purposes at the same time.

Chapter Takeaways

- Executive coaching is increasingly common because it truly works, providing an impressive ROI not only in business metrics but also in individual effectiveness.

- Executive coaches push you to fulfill your full potential. They help you clarify your goals, build on your strengths, shore up your weaknesses, overcome obstacles, stay motivated, and course correct when you get off track.

- They also reduce the chaos and overwhelm in your life by creating systems and holding you accountable.

- There's no bad time to engage a coach, but it's especially valuable when moving into a new role, facing a major obstacle, or stepping into a big opportunity.

- Choose a coach who is the right fit for your personality and goals, and don't be afraid to switch coaches if your needs change.

[5]

THE COMPOUND EFFECT: WHEN ALL THREE ELEMENTS WORK TOGETHER

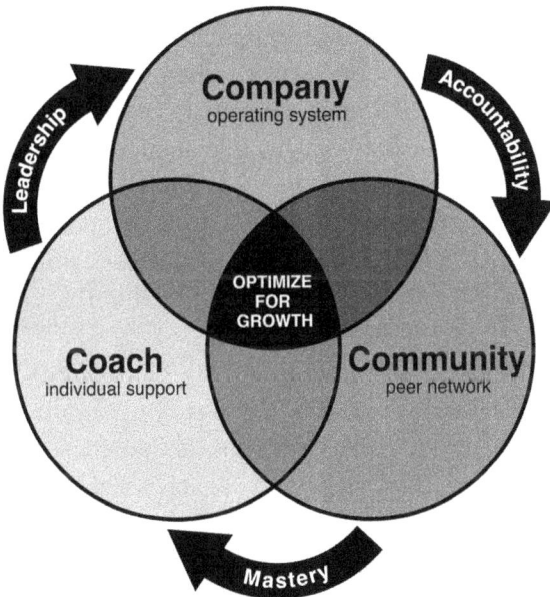

When a female executive took over the family software development business from her father in 2020, the company was at a plateau. Annual revenue was stuck at $3 million, employee turnover was at 35 percent, and the company's vision was no longer clear. However, she was determined to turn things around.

She started by implementing a company operating system. The results were solid: a 20 percent improvement in project delivery times and a reduction in employee turnover to 25 percent.

Then, she joined a peer advisory group. Through the insights on scaling and the delegation strategies learned from other CEOs, revenue doubled to $6 million, and her work week dropped from over seventy hours to fifty.

Finally, she added executive coaching. She focused on emotional intelligence, communication skills, and strategic thinking. The results were transformational: revenue reached $15 million (a 400 percent increase), employee engagement hit 8.5/10, and she now works forty-five hours per week.

Her experience demonstrates exactly what this book is all about: not the individual elements of the Optimize for Growth Model but the power of **all three together**. Each element was built upon the previous ones. The company operating system provided the foundation for implementing peer group insights. Coaching developed the leadership capabilities needed to guide the organization's growth.

Companies implementing all three elements of the Optimize for Growth Model don't just improve incrementally—they experience exponential growth. This isn't a coincidence—it's the compound, or optimization, effect in action.

All Three = Synergy

After working with hundreds of executive teams, we've seen the pattern over and over. Companies using no external support systems average 5 percent annual revenue growth. Add one element, and growth typically jumps to around 15 percent. Implement two elements, and you reach 25 percent. When all three elements work together, revenue growth can accelerate to 40 percent annually.

This synergy occurs because each element addresses different aspects of business optimization:

- **COMPANY** operating systems provide the systematic foundation for vision, accountability, and execution
- **COMMUNITY** offers a strategic perspective, external accountability, and collective wisdom
- **COACHING** develops individual leadership capabilities and personal effectiveness

When integrated properly, these elements support and amplify each other. The company operating system provides the structure to apply insights gained from peer groups and coaching. Coaching develops the leadership skills needed to implement the company operating system and build strong peer relationships. Peer groups provide accountability and insight for both system implementation and personal development commitments. Each element works better as part of the whole than on its own.

Neuroscience helps explain why integrated approaches are more effective than isolated interventions. The brain's neuroplasticity responds more effectively to multiple reinforcing stimuli than to single-source input. When leaders receive systematic frameworks (like EOS), peer learning (advisory groups), and personal development (coaching) simultaneously, neural pathways strengthen faster and more permanently.

Additionally, behavioral psychology supports the idea that multiple accountability sources create stronger motivation than a single source alone. The combination of structural accountability (company operating systems), peer accountability (advisory groups), and personal accountability (coaching) addresses different psychological drivers simultaneously.

The Integration Advantage

In our experience, companies with integrated support systems significantly outperform those using isolated approaches. The integration advantage manifests in seven key ways.

Accelerated Leadership Development: The combination of systems thinking, peer learning, and personal coaching creates well-rounded leaders faster than any single approach.

Faster Problem-Solving: When issues arise, leaders can draw from multiple resources to analyze their options and take action quickly. Company operating systems provide systematic issue resolution processes, peer groups offer diverse perspectives on similar challenges, and coaches help develop personal capabilities to address root causes.

Improved Decision Quality: Access to systematic frameworks (company operating systems like EOS), collective wisdom (community of peers), and personal insights (coaching) enables more informed, confident decisions.

Enhanced Accountability: Multiple accountability sources create powerful motivation for consistent action. Rocks provide quarterly focus, peer groups offer monthly check-ins, and coaches ensure individual development commitments are maintained.

Exponential Growth: Many companies experience exponential rather than linear growth when multiple elements are active simultaneously.

Sustainable Scalability: Unlike single-element approaches that often plateau, integrated systems adapt and scale with business growth. Each element reinforces the others, creating sustainable momentum without sacrificing quality or culture.

Cultural Transformation: The integration of all three elements fosters a culture of accountability, learning, and growth throughout the organization.

Transformational Growth

Andy Eby's journey from NFL offensive lineman to President of Bickford Senior Living is remarkable not just for its career pivot, but for the way he's fused two powerful systems—EOS (Entrepreneurial Operating System) and Stagen Leadership Academy—to create lasting impact in the senior healthcare industry.

After leaving professional football, Andy joined his family's business, Bickford Senior Living, which now operates over sixty communities nationwide. The company had a strong legacy, but as it grew, Andy and his leadership team began to feel the strain of complexity, rapid expansion, and the relentless demands of 24/7 care.

"All organizations say they live and die by the people they hire," Andy reflected. "But when you're caring for lives, and a staff member doesn't show up on the night shift, the implications of choosing the wrong person are someone's life. I had willed my company to be successful, but that was an unscalable solution."

Initially skeptical about EOS, Andy's perspective changed as he delved deeper into its principles with the guidance of Jeanet Wade, Expert EOS Implementer™. Jeanet helped Andy and his team see that willpower and hustle could only take them so far, especially as complexity grew. They needed a simple, systematic way to clarify their vision, align their leadership, and build accountability throughout the organization. "The biggest thing EOS demanded of me was to build a high-performing leadership team, because I couldn't do everything," Andy said.

Bickford Senior Living adopted EOS tools like the Scorecard, Level 10 Meetings, and the Right People/Right Seats framework. The impact was profound: "The EOS Model (with the guidance of my implementer) has transformed my organization in incredible ways. Its impact has gone beyond Bickford and has helped our industry step into a higher purpose of transforming how seniors are cared for in America," Andy shared.

While EOS provided the operational backbone, Andy sought to deepen his own leadership and that of his team. He enrolled in the Stagen Leadership Academy, known for its rigorous, purpose-driven development programs for executives. Stagen provided both coaching and community in one place, challenging Andy to lead with humility, clarity, and a deep sense of service—a perfect complement to the discipline and structure of EOS.

Through Stagen, Andy learned to integrate personal growth with organizational excellence. "When I'm at my best, I'm leading with gut love and serving from the position of a caregiver who does whatever it takes," Andy said. The Stagen experience reinforced his commitment to servant leadership and helped him weave purpose and values into every aspect of Bickford's culture.

The combination of EOS and Stagen proved transformational. EOS gave Bickford Senior Living the systems and accountability to scale sustainably, while Stagen elevated the leadership mindset and culture. Andy became not just a better operator but a more intentional, purpose-driven leader—one who could inspire his team and transform care for thousands of seniors. "This approach connects me as a leader to what's going on in my teams, even as we've scaled this multi-site, 24/7/365 business."

Andy's story, as featured on the *We Run On EOS* podcast, is a testament to the power of pairing a systematic operating framework with deep leadership development. By embracing both EOS and Stagen, Andy Eby has set a new standard for excellence in senior living—and shown that true growth happens when operational discipline meets personal purpose. Andy built not just a better business but a legacy of care and impact in his industry.

Two Ways to Implement

Through analyzing hundreds of implementations, we've identified two different approaches that maximize the compound effect.

Sequential Implementation

This approach is best for companies new to professional development.

- Start with the element addressing your biggest pain point
- Add the second element after six to twelve months of consistent progress
- Integrate the third element when the first two are functioning smoothly

Parallel Implementation

This approach is optimal for established companies ready for transformation.

- Implement all elements within twelve to twenty-four months

- Requires a higher initial investment but yields faster results
- Needs strong leadership commitment and change management

Implementation Pitfalls

Regardless of which implementation approach you choose, be sure to avoid these common mistakes:

Element Shopping: Jumping between different approaches without commitment

The longer you spend shopping, the longer it takes to start getting results. There are lots of options out there for each of the three support networks. It's okay to spend some time considering which ones are right for you. Just know that every time you switch, it's like starting over from the beginning. Do your research quickly, make a decision with confidence, and commit fully.

Partial Implementation: Using either one of the three elements or parts of each element

For example, one client dropped out of their peer group for budget reasons when they started implementing EOS. But without peer support, the CEO's confidence began to falter, as did the company's results. As soon as the CEO rejoined the peer group, his outlook changed, and with two of the three support networks in place, the company's growth began to accelerate.

Inconsistent Participation: Sporadic engagement with peer groups, coaching, or EOS sessions

As we always tell our clients, if you're not all in, you're all out. With any of the three elements—the operating system, the peer group, or the coaching—it's worse to do it halfway than to not do it at all. If you're skipping sessions, not paying attention, or not implementing the advice you're getting, you're not going to get results. You'll only waste your money and time.

Lack of Integration: Treating each element as separate rather than complementary

It's crucial that your three support systems know about each other and work together to support you. Otherwise, you will struggle with conflicting advice and accountability demands, which will only bog down your growth. For example, one client found that the goal-setting structure used by his peer group facilitator conflicted with the EOS goal system he was already using. The client was being pulled in two directions until his peer group facilitator and EOS Implementer discussed the issue and agreed on a way forward, using EOS as the vision and goal-setting system for the organization to maintain clear direction and alignment

Insufficient Investment: Under-funding any of the three elements

As we said in Chapter 1, the Optimize for Growth Model does not work with a scarcity mindset. If you're committed to truly scaling up, you must understand that a lack of investment in these support networks will dramatically slow you down. Yes, you can self-implement EOS, but you will do it exponentially faster and better if you hire a Professional/Certified/Expert Implementer. You can build your own peer network from scratch, but you'll save time and have a more valuable experience with a paid peer group. You can hire a bargain-rate coach, but you'll get better advice and grow faster with one who is experienced and truly suited to your needs.

Ultimately, the biggest pitfall is failing to pursue the Optimize for Growth Model at all.

It's easy to read this, nod your head, and then go about running your business the way you always have. But remember, companies that implement all three support systems—Company, Community, and Coaching—go further and faster than they ever could on their own.

So ask yourself: What are you risking by not implementing the Optimize for Growth Model? What opportunities will you miss? Can you afford to wait and see how things go without these support systems?

Every company faces hurdles on the path to scale. The compound effect provides the acceleration needed to break through those barriers and achieve sustainable growth. The framework has been tested time and time again, and the results are clear. The question isn't whether the compound effect works—it's whether you're ready to harness its power.

Chapter Takeaways

- When all three elements of the Optimize for Growth Model work together, they amplify each other and accelerate growth exponentially.

- This compound and optimization effect manifests in seven ways: accelerated leadership development, faster problem-solving, improved decision quality, enhanced accountability, exponential growth, sustainable scalability, and cultural transformation.

- You can implement the three elements sequentially or in parallel, depending on your company's readiness to invest and implement.

[6]

OPTIMIZE TODAY: YOUR IMPLEMENTATION ROADMAP

Throughout this book, we've shared research, case studies, and frameworks demonstrating the power of the Optimize for Growth Model. But the shift from hitting the ceiling to scaling up requires more than just information. It requires *you* to take action—to actually put in place the support structures and people you need, and to have the discipline to maintain them.

The question now is simple: what will you do first?

Building Your Compound Effect

Before taking action, you must honestly assess where you are today. This assessment determines your implementation priority and sequence in order to create the compound effect of "Optimize for Growth" in your organization.

Rate your current situation on a scale of one to five across all three areas.

COMPANY (Operating System)

1 = Never 2 = Rarely 3 = Sometimes 4 = Often 5 = Always

Does your leadership team have . . . ?	Score (1–5)
Clear vision shared by all team members	
Defined core values and culture	
A regular meeting rhythm and accountability	
Documented processes and systems	
The right people in the right seats	
Data-driven decision making	
SUM:	

COMMUNITY (Peer Network)

1 = Never 2 = Rarely 3 = Sometimes 4 = Often 5 = Always

Does your leadership team have . . . ?	Score (1–5)
Access to other business leaders	
Regular peer feedback and input	
Diverse perspectives on challenges	
A confidential environment for sharing	
Accountability from peers	
Learning from others' experiences	
SUM:	

COACH (Individual Support)

1 = Never 2 = Rarely 3 = Sometimes 4 = Often 5 = Always

Does your leadership team have ...?	Score (1–5)
Personal leadership development	
An individual accountability partner	
A skill-development focus	
An objective outside perspective	
A customized growth plan	
Regular progress reviews	
SUM:	

Your lowest scores indicate priority areas for implementation. Based on your assessment, choose your starting point:

If your COMPANY score is the lowest ...
Priority: Implement a Business Operating System

1. Take the EOS Organizational Checkup® at organizationalcheckup.com.

2. Consider hiring an EOS Implementer and schedule a complimentary ninety-minute meeting with your leadership team.

3. Choose *one* operating system and commit to implementing it (remember, you won't see results if you bounce between systems).

If your COMMUNITY score is the lowest . . .
Priority: Join a Peer Advisory Group

1. Research local peer groups (Vistage, EO, TAB, etc.).
2. Attend a trial meeting or information session.
3. Evaluate group composition and facilitation.
4. Commit to a twelve-month participation (minimum).
5. Actively engage in and contribute to discussions.

If your COACH score is the lowest . . .
Priority: Engage a Coach

1. Define your specific development goals.
2. Research qualified executive coaches.
3. Interview three to five potential coaches.
4. Establish clear success metrics.
5. Commit to a consistent meeting schedule for at least six months.

Example Action Plan

First Six Months: Foundation

- Complete assessments and review your needs
- Choose your company operating system
- Research and get referrals to operating system implementers in your area
- Begin implementation of the company operating system with your leadership team

Months Six to Twelve: Momentum

- Add a second support system (Community or Coach) if ready
- Begin roll-out of your company operating system deeper into the organization, layer by layer or department by department
- Be consistent with engagement and commitment

Over Twelve Months: Integration

- Plan the next element addition
- Evaluate progress and document lessons learned
- Plan for long-term sustainability

Optimize for Growth

- Have all three elements of Optimize for Growth (COMPANY operating system, COMMUNITY of peers, and a COACH)
- Maintain consistent participation
- Document results
- Challenge with confidence by reviewing progress and gathering feedback

Building Leadership Commitment

Implementation success requires a full commitment from the leadership team. Organizational change efforts often fail due to a lack of leadership alignment. For the Optimize for Growth Model to work, the entire leadership team must embrace the approach.

Steps to build commitment:

1. Share the research and case studies with your leadership team.
2. Conduct the assessment as a group exercise.
3. Agree on priority areas and implementation approaches.
4. Establish shared success metrics and accountability.
5. Model consistent participation and engagement.

Without leadership alignment, even the best systems and support fail to deliver results.

The Long-Term Perspective

The Optimize for Growth Model represents a long-term commitment to sustainable business development. Unlike quick fixes or flavor-of-the-month approaches, implementing all three elements of this framework builds lasting capabilities that scale with your business. The systems, relationships, and capabilities developed create sustainable competitive advantages that compound over time.

In short, this is your legacy. Companies that systematically develop operating systems, peer networks, and leadership capabilities create self-sustaining growth engines. These organizations attract better talent, serve customers more effectively, and adapt to market changes more successfully.

By implementing this model, you're not just improving current performance. You're building capabilities that will outlast your leadership tenure. You're transforming your company into an institution that will impact its community and its industry for generations.

As you begin your implementation journey, don't let perfect be the enemy of good. The best operating system implemented consistently beats the perfect system that never gets started. The right peer group that you actually attend provides more value than the ideal group you're still researching. The coach you work with regularly delivers better results than the perfect coach you never call.

Remember, real transformations take time. The goal is progress, not perfection. Start with one element and build momentum from there. The compound effect occurs when multiple elements work together, but it begins with taking the first step.

The Time Is Now

We began this book with a simple premise: the most successful entrepreneurial leaders don't grow alone. They optimize for growth by implementing three critical support systems that work in harmony to break through ceilings and achieve sustainable scale. These aren't promises—they're proven results from companies just like yours.

As we conclude, you face a fundamental choice. You can continue operating as you always have, relying on individual heroics and hoping for breakthrough results . . . or you can join the ranks of leaders who have discovered that optimization beats effort every time.

The status quo has a cost. Every quarter you remain stuck at your current ceiling represents lost revenue, missed opportunities, and accumulated frustration. The challenges that seem insurmountable today—people problems, profit pressures, control issues, and traction deficiency—will only compound over time without systematic intervention.

But the alternative is equally clear. Implementation of the Optimize for Growth Model provides a proven pathway to break through barriers and achieve sustainable growth. The research is clear, the framework is time-tested, and the resources are available to support your journey. The only remaining question is whether you'll take action. Every day you delay implementation is a day of lost growth opportunity.

Consider where your business could be eighteen months from now with the systematic implementation of all three elements. Imagine the revenue growth, improved profitability, enhanced leadership capabilities, and reduced stress that our case study companies achieved.

Now consider the cost of staying where you are. What will it cost your business, your team, and your personal satisfaction to remain stuck at your current ceiling?

The choice is yours. You can struggle alone, or you can leverage the collective wisdom and support of peers and coaches who have traveled this path.

Entrepreneurs who adopt this approach become catalysts for broader transformation. They model what's possible when leaders commit to systematic growth. They create examples that inspire others to pursue their own optimization journeys.

The question isn't whether you can succeed—it's whether you will start.

Don't grow it alone. Optimize for growth.

Let's grow!

[7]

OAR TOGETHER: CREATING PROFESSIONAL ABUNDANCE

Bonus Chapter for Trusted Business Advisors

Jonathan Jones, a Vistage Chair out of St. Louis, was familiar with the book *Traction* by Gino Wickman when he recruited two members who were already running on EOS. One was self-implemented, and the other used an out-of-town implementer. Intrigued by the model, Jonathan met with Jeanet Wade, an Expert EOS Implementer in his market, to learn more.

Within a few months, a few of Jonathan's members were working with Jeanet to implement EOS within their companies. They discovered that by having multiple Vistage members running on a similar operating system, the members had a common language. And by communicating their insights with each other (with permission), Jonathan and Jeanet both became more effective in helping their joint clients overcome major challenges. When Vistage members "graduated" from EOS implementation, Jonathan and the group continued to reinforce EOS principles and methods, helping to ensure that the system stuck.

Over the last decade, Jonathan and Jeanet have shared their expertise with over twenty clients, who have achieved remarkable outcomes, including accelerated growth, improved profitability, healthier teams, and, in many cases, successful business exits and sales. Their collaborative approach also fostered a culture of abundance—clients learned that growth was not a cut-throat solo journey but the result of leveraging community, proven systems, and expert coaching.

Their story is a testament to the power of Optimization, Abundance, and Reciprocity—or what we call "OAR Together." We've seen that Peer Advisory Chairs, Professional EOS Implementers, and Business Coaches working together, instead of in isolation, benefit everyone. Entrepreneurs get exponential value from their support professionals, who in turn build strong relationships that help sustain their practices over the long term.

The Collaboration Imperative

Traditional professional service models often create artificial competition among coaches, implementers, and peer advisory chairs. This scarcity mindset limits both client outcomes and professional growth. The OAR Together framework flips this dynamic by recognizing that each professional brings unique expertise that optimizes different aspects of business and leadership growth.

- **Optimization:** Each professional focuses on their core competency while leveraging others' strengths
- **Abundance:** There's enough business success to go around; collaboration creates more value for everyone
- **Reciprocity:** Mutual referrals and support create sustainable professional relationships

The OAR Together framework represents a fundamental shift in how entrepreneurial support professionals approach their work. By embracing these three pillars, we create ecosystems that better serve our clients while building sustainable, profitable practices. These collaborative professional relationships deliver:

- Faster client goal achievement
- Better return on total professional services investment
- Higher retention rates across all services
- Improved client satisfaction scores
- Higher revenues for support professionals

The question isn't whether to collaborate—it's how quickly you can begin building these powerful partnerships.

Optimization—Getting Clear on Roles

Effective collaboration requires a clear understanding of each professional's primary focus and optimal client fit.

EOS Implementers:

- Primary Focus: Company operating systems that align a clear vision/goals, create execution and accountability disciplines, and develop organizational health
- Typical Engagement: twenty-four months, quarterly sessions
- Best Client Stage to begin: Companies ready to systemize and scale ($1 million to $50 million)

Peer Advisory Chairs:

- Primary Focus: CEO or leader development through peer learning and external perspective
- Typical Engagement: Ongoing membership (two or more years)
- Best Client Stage: CEOs ready for peer learning (usually over $2 million in revenue)

Executive Coaches:

- Primary Focus: Individual leadership development and personal growth
- Typical Engagement: six to eighteen months, regular sessions
- Best Client Stage: Leaders ready for personal development (any business size)

This clarity prevents role confusion while highlighting complementary strengths. Rather than competing for the same clients, professionals can focus on their expertise areas while referring clients to appropriate partners.

The following matrix summarizes the areas where each role is best equipped to add value. This helps professionals understand when to engage others and which pathways create optimal client outcomes.

The Complementary Strengths Matrix

Challenge Area	EOS Implementer	Peer Chair	Executive Coach
Vision Clarity	★ ★ ★	★	★ ★
Team Issues	★ ★ ★	★ ★	★ ★
Process and Execution	★ ★ ★	★	★ ★
Leadership Development	★ ★	★ ★	★ ★ ★
Strategic Thinking	★ ★ ★	★ ★	★ ★
Personal Growth	★	★ ★	★ ★ ★
Accountability	★ ★ ★	★	★ ★
Network Building	★	★ ★ ★	★

Successful professional partnerships typically follow this sequence:

1. First, an EOS Implementer works with the company's leadership team to establish the company operating system - the way goals are set, execution of vision is accomplished, people stay connected and meet, leaders and managers get accountability, and decisions are made.

2. Then, a Peer Advisory Chair adds an external perspective through peer group facilitation.

3. Finally, an Executive Coach steps in to develop individual leadership capabilities and readiness.

Abundance—Creating a Collaborative Mindset

We stated in Chapter 1 that for the Optimize for Growth Model to be effective, business leaders must adopt an abundance mindset. The same goes for their support professionals. You can only OAR Together from a place of abundance—otherwise, you'll only undermine your client's ability to build the three mutually-reinforcing support networks they need.

Scarcity Mindset:

- Viewing other professionals as threats
- Hoarding client relationships
- Avoiding referrals due to competition fears
- Focusing on individual success only

Abundance Mindset:

- Seeing other professionals as potential partners
- Sharing opportunities and resources
- Making referrals based on the clients' best interests
- Celebrating collective success

Remember, it's not a question of either/or. If you're an executive coach, you're not competing with your client's peer group facilitator or EOS Implementer (and vice versa). Your client needs *all* of you. More than that, they need you to work *together* to create a united front of strategic direction and accountability. Collaborating creates better results for them, which leads to better results for you and your business in the long run.

Reciprocity—Building Collaboration Networks

Creating effective professional partnerships requires intentional relationship building:

- Identify potential collaboration partners in your area

- Attend each other's events and programs
- Develop mutual understanding of approaches and philosophies
- Establish referral criteria and processes

Successful collaboration requires clear ethical boundaries and practices:

- Client Confidentiality:
    - Always obtain explicit client permission before discussing cases
    - Share only the relevant information needed for effective collaboration
    - Respect the unique confidentiality requirements of each profession

- Professional Boundaries:
    - Clearly define roles and responsibilities for each professional
    - Avoid scope creep into other professionals' areas of expertise
    - Refer clients when issues fall outside your competency
    - Maintain professional independence while collaborating
    - Emphasize an abundance mindset and client success over individual professional gain

Remember: The goal of collaboration isn't to blur professional boundaries but to create clear pathways for clients to access the full spectrum of support they need to achieve sustainable growth and success. When EOS Implementers, Peer Advisory Chairs, and Executive Coaches work together, they create an ecosystem that serves clients better than isolated approaches. This collaboration creates abundance for all parties while focusing on client success. The OAR Together framework (Optimization, Abundance, Reciprocity) provides a structure for professional partnerships that amplifies the effect.

RESOURCES

Ready to begin your optimization journey? Contact us at:

- Jonathan B. Smith: eosworldwide.com/jonathan-smith or staycuriousjbs.com
- Jeanet L. Wade: eosworldwide.com/jeanet-wade or business-alchemist.com

For speaking engagements:

- Jonathan B. Smith: staycuriousjbs.com
- Jeanet L. Wade: business-alchemist.com/speaking-workshops

There are many resources for each element of the Optimize for Growth Model. Below are just a few of the ones we've encountered on our journey.

COMPANY Operating Systems

We are, of course, partial to EOS. The Entrepreneurial Operating System® (EOS) is a complete set of simple concepts and practical tools that has helped thousands of entrepreneurs around the world get what they want from their businesses. Implementing the EOS Model, toolbox, and process will help you and your leadership team improve in three key areas: Vision, Traction, and Healthy. By creating a healthy, cohesive, and high-trust organization, you'll gain traction (accountability and execution) on your vision (strategy, focus, and planning) in a proven, consistent, and scalable way over the many phases and lifecycles of your business.

Since the creation of EOS in the early 2000s, other operating systems or approaches have been developed. Some focus on only strategy creation. Others look at organizational effectiveness through processes and data. Some are centered around financial acumen and financial goal-setting. Be sure to determine the right fit for your organization's short-term and long-term needs so that you are getting a holistic and sustainable solution for running an effective organization.

Since some of these are considered competitive to EOS, we will refrain from description or commentary so that you can independently research and decide what's best for you and your organization. Remember, you must choose *one* operating system for your business to be effective; you can't run on multiple.

- **Entrepreneurial Operating System (EOS):** Visit EOSworldwide.com to take the Organizational Checkup, find a local EOS Implementer, or get valuable content (blogs and books, like *Traction* by Gino Wickman).

- Scaling Up (Rockefeller Habits)

- OKRs (Objectives and Key Results)

- 4 Disciplines of Execution (4DX)

- Great Game of Business

COMMUNITY and Peer Advisory Groups

- **The Alternative Board (TAB):** Peer advisory boards for small and medium-sized business owners, with groups in over twenty countries. Monthly meetings and executive coaching. thealternativeboard.com

- **Birthing of Giants:** A fellowship and peer-coaching organization for middle-market business owners, designed to accelerate strategic growth through expert-led curriculum, peer accountability, and real-world mentorship. birthingofgiants.com

- **Bunker Labs:** A non-profit initiative that empowers military veterans and military spouses to launch and grow businesses. ivmf.syracuse.edu/programs/entrepreneurship/bunker-labs/

- **C12:** A group for Christian CEOs and business owners that integrates business excellence with biblical **principles.** joinc12.com

- **CEO Roundtable:** Peer advisory groups for mid-sized company CEOs and funded startup founders, primarily in the US. Confidential groups of eight to twelve members, with monthly meetings. ceo-roundtable.com

- **Chief Executive Boards International:** Local CEO peer groups in the U.S. Midwest and Southeast.

- **Chief Executive Network (CEN):** Peer groups for CEOs of mid-market companies (manufacturing, tech, services, etc.) in North America. Focused on benchmarking, best practices, and confidential advice. chiefexecutivenetwork.com

- **Convene:** Peer advisory groups for Christian CEOs and business owners, primarily in the US. Focused on business excellence and faith-based leadership. convenenow.com

- **Entrepreneurs' Organization (EO):** Global network for entrepreneurs and business owners with over 18,000 members in more than sixty countries. Forum-based peer groups, executive education, and global events. eonetwork.org

- **Founder OS:** A modern, curated peer group and support platform for venture-backed startup founders, offering structured programs, facilitated sessions, and frameworks for scaling leadership. founderos.com

- **G100:** Invite-only, exclusive peer learning and networking for CEOs and CXOs of billion-dollar companies. Features executive education and access to industry leaders. g100.com

- **Hampton:** An exclusive membership community for founders and CEOs of high-growth, tech-focused startups. joinhampton.com

- **Helm:** Ultra-personalized CEO peer groups for problem-solving and business growth. helmclub.co

- **Leadership Council:** Designed by one of the original forum format co-creators, Leadership Council focuses on executive leaders by facilitating expertly moderated, conflict-free monthly peer advisory groups of up to twelve executives. leadershipcouncilstl.com

- **Renaissance Executive Forums (REF):** A global organization with over 3,000 members in twenty countries (Americas, Europe, Asia). Confidential peer advisory boards for business leaders, facilitated by certified Forum Leaders. ref.global

- **Tiger 21:** A global peer membership organization for high-net-worth wealth creators and investors, typically with more than $10 million in investable assets. tiger21.com

- **Vistage:** The world's largest CEO peer advisory and executive coaching organization with over 45,000 members in more than forty countries. Monthly confidential peer group meetings for CEOs, business owners, and key executives. vistage.com

- **Women Presidents Organization (WPO):** For women presidents of multimillion-dollar companies with chapters worldwide.

- **Young Presidents' Organization (YPO):** Prestigious global network for CEOs and presidents under age forty-five with 35,000+ members in 140+ countries. Offers peer forums, events, and leadership development. ypo.org

- **Industry- and Region-Specific Peer Groups:** Many industries and regions have their own networks, such as industry-specific CEO councils, local Chambers of Commerce, CEO forums, and regional executive roundtables

COACHES

Be sure to interview multiple candidates and check credentials and experience.

- Brian Tracy Coaching: briantracy.com
- Chapman & Co. Leadership Institute: ccoleadership.com
- Dixie Gillaspie: dixiegillaspie.com
- Executive Coach Group: executivecoachgroup.com
- Perfect Aim: rodneymueller.com
- Positive Intelligence Coaches: web.positiveintelligence.com/saboteurs-derailing-traction
- Small Business Coach Associates: smallbusinesscoach.org
- Stagen Leadership: stagen.com
- Stewart Leadership: stewartleadership.com
- Strategic Coach: strategiccoach.com
- Tony Robbins Results Coaching: tonyrobbins.com/business-coaching
- Vivid Performance Group: vividperformancegroup.com

Where to Find More Coaches

- Ask your network for a referral
- Noomii Executive Coach Directory: www.noomii.com
- International Coach Federation: www.coachfederation.org

ENDNOTES

1   This model was originally introduced in Jonathan B. Smith's short book *Optimize for Growth*, published in 2015. This book is an expansion of that content, with additional details, concepts, examples, and case studies.

2   Dan Bigman, "Why You Need a CEO Peer Group. Now.," ChiefExecutive.net, March 8, 2023, https://chiefexecutive. net/why-you-need-a-ceo-peer-group-now/.

3   Peter A. Thiel and Blake Masters, *Zero to One: Notes on Startups, or How to Build the Future* (New York, NY: Crown Business, 2014).

4   Gallup, "State of the Global Workplace," Gallup.com, May 14, 2019, https://www.gallup.com/workplace/257552/ state-global-workplace-2017.aspx.

5   Michael Guta, "82% of Business Failure Is Due to Poor Cash Management (Infographic)," Small Business Trends, October 14, 2019, https://smallbiztrends.com/ small-business-funding-statistics/.

6   Global Board and CEO Practice, "Measure of Leadership: CEOS and Directors on Navigating Change," Spencer Stuart, June 2024, https://www.spencerstuart.com/ research-and-insight/measure-of-leadership-ceos-and- directors-on-navigating-change.

7   Boris Ewenstein, Wesley Smith, and Ashvin Sologar, "Changing Change Management," McKinsey & Company, July 1, 2015, https:// www.mckinsey.com/featured-insights/leadership/ changing-change-management.

8   Fernando F. Suarez and Juan S. Montes, "Building Organizational Resilience," Harvard Business Review, November 1, 2020, https://hbr.org/2020/11/building-organizational-resilience.

9   Larry E. Greiner, Evolution and Revolution as Organizations Grow. In L. Mainiero & C. Tromley (Eds.), *Developing Managerial Skills in Organizational Behavior: Exercises, Cases, and Readings (2nd ed.)* (pp. 322–329). Prentice Hall. (1994)

10 James C. Collins and Morten T. Hansen, *Great by Choice: Uncertainty, Chaos, and Luck: Why Some Thrive despite Them All* (New York, NY: HarperCollins Publishers, 2011).

11 Deborah Grayson Riegel, "8 Ways Leaders Delegate Successfully," Harvard Business Review, November 16, 2023, https://hbr.org/2019/08/8-ways-leaders-delegate-successfully.

12 Ankur Agrawal, Mark Khavkin, and Jonathan Slonim, "Bringing a Real-World Edge to Forecasting," McKinsey & Company, March 13, 2020, https://www.mckinsey.com/capabilities/strategy-and-corporate-finance/our-insights/bringing-a-real-world-edge-to-forecasting.

13 "Repeatable Models: The Key to Achieving 'Good Scale,'" Bain & Company, November 2014, https://www.bain.com/insights/growing-prosperity-chapter-4/.

14 "Organize to Value," McKinsey & Company, accessed June 18, 2025, https://www.mckinsey.com/capabilities/people-and-organizational-performance/how-we-help-clients/organize-to-value.

15 If this story sounds familiar, you probably remember it from Gino Wickman's book, *Traction* (page 51).

16 Joe Nocera, "Ford's Turnaround Carries Lessons for G.M.," The New York Times, June 28, 2014, https://

www.nytimes.com/2014/06/28/opinion/joe-nocera-fords-turnaround-carries-lessons-for-gm.html.

17 Rocks are big, important tasks that need to be accomplished in the next 90 days. More on that later in this chapter.

18 Dan Bigman, "Why You Need a CEO Peer Group. Now.," ChiefExecutive.net, March 8, 2023, https://chiefexecutive.net/why-you-need-a-ceo-peer-group-now/.

19 Andrew Feghali, " Executive Peer Advisory Groups: Who They Are? What Are Their Benefits? Why Do Members Join and Stay?," University of San Diego, May 22, 2022, https://digital.sandiego.edu/cgi/viewcontent.cgi?article=1935&context=dissertations.

20 Carolyn Dewar et al., "The CEO Moment: Leadership for a New Era," McKinsey & Company, July 21, 2020, https://www.mckinsey.com/featured-insights/leadership/the-ceo-moment-leadership-for-a-new-era.

21 Eric Schmidt, "Everybody Needs a Coach," YouTube, 2009, https://youtu.be/aVKPlS0ejtk.

22 International Coach Federation, "ICF Global Coaching Client Study," ICF - Search Research Portal, April 2009, https://researchportal.coachingfederation.org/Document/Pdf/abstract_190.

23 Jack J. Phillips, "Measuring the Roi of a Coaching Intervention, Part 2," *Performance Improvement* 46, no. 10 (2007): 10–23, https://doi.org/10.1002/pfi.167.

24 Andreea Nicolau et al., "The Effects of Executive Coaching on Behaviors, Attitudes, and Personal Characteristics: A Meta-Analysis of Randomized Control Trial Studies," *Frontiers in Psychology* 14 (June 2, 2023), https://doi.org/10.3389/fpsyg.2023.1089797.

25 International Coach Federation. *International Coach Federation Global Client Coaching Study.*

26 International Coach Federation. *International Coach Federation Global Client Coaching Study.*
27 InsideOut Development, "Building a Coaching Culture That Drives Results and Grows People," InsideOut Development, 2023, https://insideoutdev.com/hubfs/Resources%20Website%202023/White%20Papers/a-framework-for-building-a-coaching-culture.pdf?hsLang=en.
28 1. Jean O'Toole, "Trends in Executive Coaching: Is There Demand in 2024?," iNLP Center, January 24, 2024, https://inlpcenter.org/trends-in-executive-coaching/.

Jonathan B. Smith

Jonathan B. Smith is a renowned entrepreneur, author, and Expert EOS Implementer® who has dedicated his career to helping growth-minded business leaders achieve clarity, traction, and results. As one of the earliest clients of Gino Wickman—the creator of the Entrepreneurial Operating System (EOS)—Jonathan experienced firsthand the power of a systematic approach to business transformation, a story featured in the pages of Traction itself.

Jonathan's entrepreneurial journey began with founding and growing multiple companies, including serving as COO of Wave Dispersion Technologies, where he led the business from startup to a global provider of maritime security solutions. It was during this period that Jonathan met Gino Wickman through the Entrepreneurs' Organization in Detroit. At a time when EOS was still in its infancy, Jonathan and his brother became some of Gino's very first clients, helping to shape what would become the world-renowned EOS framework. This early adoption not only transformed Jonathan's own business but also ignited his passion for helping other leaders break through their growth ceilings.

Since 2013, Jonathan has facilitated over 1,000 EOS sessions with more than 125 entrepreneurial companies, guiding leadership teams to align vision, strengthen accountability, and build self-managing organizations. His clients have achieved over 25 successful business exits, a testament to his expertise in strategy, execution, and leadership development. Jonathan is known for his practical, servant-leadership style—focusing on the greater mission and empowering teams to achieve what they once thought impossible.

In addition to his EOS work, Jonathan is a Negotiations Trainer and Coach with The Black Swan Group, working closely with former FBI hostage negotiator Chris Voss. He brings unique expertise in negotiation, tactical empathy, and high-stakes communication to his clients. Jonathan also serves on the Advisory Board of the International Spy Museum and the Investment Committee of TF Investors, a private equity fund investing exclusively in EOS-run companies.

A commercial pilot, dog trainer, and avid offshore fisherman, Jonathan brings curiosity and a spirit of adventure to both his professional and personal pursuits. His true passion is helping others believe they can achieve what they once thought was impossible—one system, one conversation, and one breakthrough at a time.

Jeanet L. Wade

Jeanet L. Wade is recognized as an Expert EOS Implementer®, a dynamic business consultant, and the best-selling Forbes Books author of *The Human Team: So, You Created a Team But People Showed Up!* As the founder of Business Alchemist, Jeanet has dedicated her career, spanning over twenty-five years, to helping entrepreneurial leadership teams simplify complexity, align around a shared vision, and achieve breakthrough results.

With a background spanning marketing, innovation management, and executive strategy, Jeanet's journey began in the corporate world, where she led teams at Maritz, Inc. and American Express Incentive Services. These formative experiences ignited her passion for unlocking human potential and building healthy, high-performing teams. After witnessing firsthand the challenges of rapid growth and misaligned teams, she pivoted to consulting and coaching, founding her own firm to help organizations harness the power of people-focused leadership.

Since 2013, Jeanet has facilitated, taught, and coached the Entrepreneurial Operating System® (EOS®). Her approach blends strategic insight with a practical, action-oriented framework, enabling leaders to get "Traction®" on their vision, foster accountability, and create environments where both people and profits thrive. Jeanet's reputation as the go-to resource for effective, healthy team dynamics has earned her accolades, including being named one of the "Top 100 St. Louisans to Know to Succeed in Business" by St. Louis Small Business Monthly.

A passionate advocate for people-first leadership, Jeanet's book, *The Human Team*, introduces her groundbreaking framework, The 6 Facets of Human Needs®, which helps leaders understand and meet the essential needs of their teams—Confidence, Clarity, Connection, Contribution, Challenge, and Consideration. Her work empowers organizations to maximize their "Return on Individual" and achieve lasting, people-powered growth.

Jeanet is available for interviews, workshops, and presentations on leading healthy teams and driving unprecedented business growth. Learn more at Business-Alchemist.com or connect with her on LinkedIn.

A UNIFIED TEAM CREATES OPERATIONAL EFFICIENCY & MEASURABLE ROI

Book Jeanet for your next event for a presentation or workshop that will help leaders, executives and entrepreneurs learn a quick and simple path to success and get their company unified on direction.

START THE CONVERSATION TODAY

Business-Alchemist.com

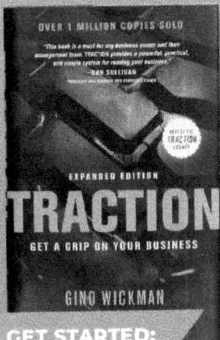

THE TRACTION LIBRARY™

GETTING EVERYONE IN YOUR COMPANY ON THE SAME PAGE

TRACTION: GET A GRIP ON YOUR BUSINESS
Strengthen the Six Key Components® of your business using simple yet powerful tools and disciplines.

FOR EVERYONE

GET STARTED:

ROCKET FUEL: THE ONE ESSENTIAL COMBINATION
Dive into how the Visionary and Integrator duo can take their company to new heights.

FOR VISIONARIES & INTEGRATORS

GET A GRIP: AN ENTREPRENEURIAL FABLE
Follow this fable's characters as they learn how to run on EOS® and address real-world business situations.

FOR THE LEADERSHIP TEAM

WHAT THE HECK IS EOS?
Create ownership and buy-in from every employee in your organization, inspiring them to take an active role in achieving your company's vision.

FOR ALL EMPLOYEES, MANAGERS, & SUPERVISORS

HOW TO BE A GREAT BOSS!
Help bosses at all levels of your organization get the most from their people.

FOR LEADERS, MANAGERS, & SUPERVISORS

THE EOS LIFE
Learn how to create your ideal life by doing what you love, with people you love, making a huge difference, being compensated appropriately, and with time for other passions.

FOR ENTREPRENEURS & LEADERSHIP TEAMS

EOS

THE EOS MASTERY SERIES™
Dive deeper into each of the Six Key Components® for more masterful execution.

EOSWORLDWIDE.COM

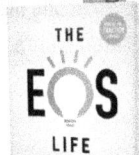

THIS BOOK IS PROTECTED INTELLECTUAL PROPERTY

Instant IP [IP]

The author of this book values Intellectual Property. The book you just read is protected by Instant IP[IP], a proprietary process, which integrates blockchain technology giving Intellectual Property "Global Protection." By creating a "Time-Stamped" smart contract that can never be tampered with or changed, we establish "First Use" that tracks back to the author.

Instant IP [IP] functions much like a Pre-Patent since it provides an immutable "First Use" of the Intellectual Property. This is achieved through our proprietary process of leveraging blockchain technology and smart contracts. As a result, proving "First Use" is simple through a global and verifiable smart contract. By protecting intellectual property with blockchain technology and smart contracts, we establish a "First to File" event.

Protected by Instant IP [IP]

LEARN MORE AT INSTANTIP.TODAY